Luscious
LIQUEURS

50 Recipes for Sublime and Spirited Infusions to Sip and Savor

---

A.J. RATHBUN

PHOTOGRAPHY BY MELISSA PUNCH

The Harvard Common Press
Boston, Massachusetts

FOR MY GRANDMOTHER GERTRUDE MIDDENDORF, WHO TAUGHT ME AT AN EARLY AGE THE IMPORTANCE OF A GOOD DRINK

The Harvard Common Press
535 Albany Street
Boston, Massachusetts 02118
www.harvardcommonpress.com

Printed in China
Printed on acid-free paper

Library of Congress Cataloging-in-Publication Data
Rathbun, A. J. (Arthur John), 1969-
   Luscious liqueurs : 50 recipes for sublime and spirited infusions to sip and savor / A.J. Rathbun.
      p. cm.
   Includes index.
   ISBN 978-1-55832-380-3 (hardcover)
   1. Liqueurs. 2. Cocktails. I. Title.
   TP611.R38 2008
   641.2'55--dc22
                                          2008003085

Special bulk-order discounts are available on this and other Harvard Common Press books. Companies and organizations may purchase books for premiums or resale, or may arrange a custom edition, by contacting the Marketing Director at the address above.

Book design by Elizabeth Van Itallie
Photographs by Melissa Punch
Food and drink styling by Brian Preston-Campbell
Prop styling by Lauren Anne Niles
Author photographs by Natalie Fuller

10 9 8 7 6 5 4 3 2 1

CONTENTS

INTRODUCTION

Being a host or hostess at a swank soirée, a pleasant party, or a wild wingding should be, and usually is, a joyous thing. Much like giving someone a grand gift, throwing a fun celebration for any old reason (the first day of spring, President Taft's birthday, the anniversary of the release of Bruce Lee's classic *Enter the Dragon*) is a present for you and for the attendees. Serving up whatever signature drink you've decided on, and watching guests' smiles start to shine when they taste it (whether it's something new or a venerable mix), instills a lovely feeling. Life is right.

Now, multiply that feeling times ten (or imagine it multiplied). That feeling is what happens when you serve up that first drink and catch a view of that first satisfied smile when the drink you're serving contains a liqueur you've made yourself. It's amazing—not only did you make the drink, but at least some, if not all, of the ingredients within the drink. You move, rapidly, from the realm of dandy host or hostess into the immortal realm of host-or-hostess-with-the-mostest. It's a realm that, once you've discovered it, you'll never want to leave—and with this book by your side, you'll never have to.

ACKNOWLEDGMENTS

T o make a liqueur that boasts deep body, layers of flavor, and sometimes a sweet, silly side, it takes not only a bit of time and effort, but also the right ingredients. In the same manner, putting this book together included a number of different human ingredients, and I'd like to say thanks to each of those ingredients, with a couple of extra-smooth call-outs to a few standouts, starting with Valerie Cimino, my editor at The Harvard Common Press. Here's to you, Valerie, for your immeasurable help in taking this idea from a bunch of scattered components to a classy and luscious cordial. From start to finish, it's been a blast. Thanks and cheers also to every single member of the HCP staff. If only the interstate liquor laws would let me send homemade liqueurs through the mail, you each would have bottles and bottles of my finest creations on your desks—but since I can't send them, let me just say thanks again, and again, for all the help. Thanks also to Melissa Punch, drink photographer extraordinaire.

A whole case of thanks also goes to my agent Michael Bourret, who is a stylish bottle of limoncello all on his own, with his bursts of citrus-like imagination and his combination of sweetness and strength. My

copious thanks may become rather like an oft-heard refrain, but should never be thought of as any less than heartfelt, because you've been amazing throughout this whole process.

Speaking of amazing, no pal was more amazingly helpful in my world of liqueur-book writing than the Husky Boy, Jeremy Holt, who not only provided the recipe for the Hot Horse, but who also is a liqueur master willing to share his ideas, expertise, and (best of all) end results. Thanks again, my man, for everything. Also, thanks to the many, many liqueur testers for being so willing to sip what's put in front of you— you're my kind of people, and your opinions and ideas were and are great. Thanks to all who've taken sips along the way, with special shout-outs to Matt and Maile, Rebecca and Eric, Megan, Andy and Deena, Mark and Leslie, Brad and Christy, Kyla and Mike, and the whole Kitchen-Edit crew (I'm toasting to you, Alexis, Andrea, Katherine, Kelly, and Scott), who always were great when I'd bring the infusions into the office for testing and tasting, and thanks also to the whole Fuller family, and my mom, Trudy; dad, Art; and stepmom, Theresa.

Liqueurs need to have the right music played to them, or they turn out a bit sour. My liqueurs' soundtrack during the writing of this book was a bubbling mix of the Withholders, the Malinks, the Rich Yarges Experience, The National Trust, the DGRE, GFB, Arthur Dodge and those Horsefeathers, Tales from the Birdbath, and the Belles.

The last sip and the last thanks go out to my wife, Natalie, who besides coming up with many liqueur ideas and many cocktail ideas to go with the liqueurs, and keeping the Sookie-dog from spilling the liqueurs (though who can blame Sookie—she wanted a taste of the tasty mixes, too), never seemed to mind when I turned the basement into a liqueur laboratory. I'll be sure to chill the citrus mixes and save the final drop of the Sweet Macadamiana for you.

LIQUEUR BASICS

Home entertaining is as special now as it was during the 1920s, when everyone had elegant glassware and sharp outfits and when creative cocktails and homemade delicacies were the norm, not the rarity. The difference today is that the attitude is more a combination of fun and homey, without some of the class-conscious stuffiness of the past. But the modern wide range of party populists like you should still be looking for something to set your affairs above the everyday, something to show off your ability to create culinary and cocktail masterpieces as well as attractive party environments, all on your own. Homemade liqueurs take your party to the next level.

But the liqueurs in this book aren't just for unveiling in drinks or solo at parties. You'll get that same satisfied feeling when a friend, family member, or paramour opens a gift you've presented to find a bottle of homemade liqueur inside—and when the recipient takes that first sip and "oohs" and "ahhs" at your ability and perseverance in making such a nectar. Also, if you show up at a party with a bottle of homemade liqueur as a present for the hosts, you automatically become the favorite guest (a position that may just ensure you get first dibs at the snack buffet), and you also become the guest that tops the invite list for future parties. And that, friends, is a prime position, one you want to occupy.

The liqueurs in this book aren't just for giving, either. Though they work perfectly as the centerpiece of any rocking revelry, and as gifts for all occasions, they also are wonderfully fun to make and keep for yourself (it's perfectly fine to be a little selfish). After a hard day of work or play, coming home to pour yourself a tall (or short) glass of a liqueur you've created by hand, that you've raised patiently over the weeks, that you've crafted with care (and maybe even sung, or at least crooned, to once or twice)—that liqueur tastes so fine, and makes any moment memorable, even if you're sitting alone on the back porch toasting the sun as it creeps below the horizon.

This book, and the liqueurs contained herein, are at heart for those who love all the moments mentioned above, who like to entertain and be entertained, and who like cooking and cocktailing at home as well as out and about—the cocktail-loving soirée set that boasts of multiple entertaining influences, from Mom to today's top chefs. Basically, it's for you. The mixes inside might take a little time to create, but the end results are delicious and look great. From citrus smackers and fruit flavors to spicy mergers to exotic mixes to sweet after-dinner treats, they transcend the offerings from typical liquor stores. Combined with tips, gifting ideas, and suggestions for fabulous cocktails, they're also shaken with a large of dose of merriment. Like a guest at a party, this book's a fun companion, and once you open it up and invite it around, you'll soon find your kitchen transformed into a hopping liqueur-making habitat. Because—and I say this from experience—once you start making liqueurs it becomes a bit of an addiction, albeit an awfully tasty one.

I chose the recipes contained within first and foremost because I think they taste wonderful. After much testing and trials and tribulations (the trouble I'll go through for you), and a little help with tasting and trying out recipes from liqueur-loving family, friends, and coworkers, I narrowed the list down to 50 recipes. All can be sipped solo, and most also work well when combined with other liquids to make cocktails—a number of the liqueurs even go well in savory and sweet edibles. The fun doesn't stop when the liqueur's been strained, folks.

I also tried to provide a range of recipes, on two levels. First, a range of tastes and ingredients, to ensure that the book holds something for everyone who reads it, whether you like your liqueurs with a little bitter or herbal backbone or you're looking for something to satisfy the sweet tooth that's always whispering to you. Second, a range of different liqueur-constructing techniques, with some recipes that need chopping of nuts, some that need muddling of leaves, some that need blending and chilling, and some that need hardly any help at all to get the flavor-infusing party started. Once you dive into the process and taste the recipes here, you'll be able to branch out if you want.

This brings up a final introductory point: Stop waiting around. Although the recipes are easy to prepare, these liqueurs do, for the most part, need time to infuse before being served, so I suggest you stock up your liqueur laboratory, start browsing the recipes, pick a mix that will tickle your taste buds, and start creating—and enjoying—your own homemade liqueur masterpieces.

THE LIQUEUR LABORATORY

S ipping a luscious liqueur that you've created with your own hands is a fantastic feeling. (Serving one to a friend, family member, or spouse who praises the liqueur after the first sip is a pretty great feeling, too.) Luckily, the creation of liqueurs and cordials at home isn't nearly as hard as you might think. But, as in many types of creation, a little proper prior planning makes everything go much more easily. The following pages, taken in slowly and carefully, like a glass of chilled Limoncello on a summer's day, will help you prepare to become a master of making your own.

Very Important Vessels for Making and Storing

While many of the actual ingredients in the recipes can and should be bought close to when you're going to start stirring and storing, there are a number of items that you'll want around beforehand, items to hang on to throughout the mixing of many different liqueurs. When setting up your lab or pulling together your set of liqueur-making tools, the first, and maybe most important, will be at least one, and very likely several, large and sturdy glass jars with tight-fitting lids. I tend toward having 2- to 3-gallon-size glass jars, because they accommodate all different recipes. While I have a few smaller jars around to use for smaller recipes, there's really no reason if you have the space not to pony up for the larger ones. Most liqueurs need a little swirling during those long weeks of waiting, and a good-size jar makes this really easy; it also ensures that you don't realize a jar's too small in the middle of putting a recipe together.

Related to the mixing jars are the final receptacles you're going to strain the liqueurs into once they're done. I use a lot of 750-milliliter Lorina bottles (which come with tasty lemonade in them—not a bad bonus) for this purpose, for a couple of reasons. First, their labels wash off easily and don't leave a lot of sticky residue. Second, this size of Lorina bottle has the swing top with a ceramic and rubber stopper that seals tightly. Third, they're big enough to hold a lot of liquid—about 1⅔ pints—but small enough to not overwhelm the freezer if chilling is needed, or the bar shelf if it isn't. Finally, they look darn pretty, which is important if you'll be giving away a bottle of liqueur as a gift. But there are a number of other bottles you can use for final storing purposes, including old liquor bottles, canning jars, or any decorative bottles with secure lids. The latter you can find in gift shops, sometimes food shops, and even at garage and yard sales. Hunting out interesting, attractive bottles is oodles of fun. But to underline two points: Make sure you wash them thoroughly before using, and make sure they have *really* secure lids. Spilling a liqueur you've been waiting a month to try is heartbreaking. Trust me.

Mighty Tools of the Liqueur Trade

Jars and bottles are crucial, but you'll find there are some other tools you'll use just as much (if not for as long a period of time). Perhaps at the top of the tool list are two items that might at first glance seem slight when stacked against those kitchen tools one usually sees as "mighty." These two are a sturdy little funnel and cheesecloth, and they go together when making liqueur like homemade banana liqueur goes with crème de cacao. When straining the liqueurs to rid them of debris from ingredients, you usually go from large glass container to pitcher to bottle, sometimes repeating the last step more than once. At each step, the pouring is done through cheesecloth, and usually a funnel is involved, too (especially when pouring into those decorative bottles). I've tried a number of different brands of cheesecloth, and have had the same success with each, so just pick up whatever your local grocery store offers. When investing in a funnel, be sure to get one that fits into the bottles you're using, but doesn't have such a tiny point as to make straining impossible. If you do get one that's too small, sometimes just cutting off the end helps, as they tend to taper.

On the other end of the spectrum, at the beginning of the liqueur-making process, you'll find that a really sharp knife and a good cutting board are indispensable for peeling and cutting fruit and herbs. Depending on your knife skills, a sharp peeler may end up being your best friend when taking the peel off of citrus fruits. In addition, I find that a mortar and pestle come in very handy when crushing spices to extract maximum flavor, though you can use a sturdy wooden spoon and a bowl in a pinch. And speaking of spoons, there's a lot of stirring in these pages, so don't start without a long-handled wooden or metal spoon at close reach. While you can use a spoon for mashing up herbs and such in a container (to release their oils), getting a good muddler, which is specifically designed for this action, isn't a bad idea. Other convenient tools include a good set of measuring devices, both spoons and cups, clean towels (liqueurs get sticky), and a small glass cup for tasting (the last isn't really a tool, but it's sure helpful).

The Liquor Makes the Liqueur

With all this talk about homemade liqueurs, it's possible to overlook the liquor that provides the base upon which classy cordials are constructed. In this book you'll find liqueurs made with vodka, grain alcohol, rum, brandy, and even Scotch. Vodka may be the most prevalent (since its neutral nature makes it an attractive playmate for other flavors), but the others also are interesting and enjoyable bases to build on in different situations. When picking out your base liquor, remember that there isn't a recipe in here that doesn't mix that liquor with other things: There are no vodka-on-the-rocks liqueurs. This means that if you're purchasing an ultra-top-shelf brandy, or vodka, or any of the other bases, you probably want to keep that to sip solo, or without a lot of other flavorings. For the liqueur-making, you don't want rotgut but a nice, midrange base liquor, one that isn't preflavored, and one that isn't going to shock you with the price. I tend to purchase the bigger bottles whenever possible, because then I get to make multiple liqueurs without taking multiple trips to the liquor store (not that those trips aren't a good time), and because those large bottles tend to be better deals.

For some recipes, you'll see grain alcohol—a very high-proof, twice-distilled, flavorless alcohol—used as the base. A common brand is Everclear. Grain alcohol is not available in every state, so if you live in a state where you can't purchase it, simply sub in the highest-proof vodka you can find. I'm not saying it's going to be perfect, but your liqueur will still be darn tasty.

SIMPLE SYRUP
Makes about 4½ pints

Though it's not liquor, simple syrup is perhaps even more important in these recipes, as it's an ingredient found in nearly all of them. Some liqueurs have special syrups (using brown sugar, for example), and instructions to make these not-quite-as-simple-syrups are detailed in the specific recipes that use them. But when a liqueur just calls for an amount of basic simple syrup, use this recipe. I like to have simple syrup around at all times, for liqueurs, for cocktails, and for lemonade and other drinks. It's easy to make and stores well in the refrigerator. Having simple syrup around also means that you don't have to rush a batch when you realize you're at the simple syrup step in one of the liqueur recipes.

2½ cups water

3 cups sugar

1. Combine the sugar and water in a medium-size saucepan. Stirring occasionally, bring the mixture to a boil over medium-high heat. Lower the heat a bit, and keep the mixture at a low boil for 5 minutes.

2. Turn off the heat, and let the syrup completely cool in the pan. Store in a clean glass jar in the refrigerator for up to 1 month.

The Fresh Factor

One of the more obvious goals when concocting your own liqueurs is to make them taste as good as possible. This doesn't mean that every liqueur is then going to be loved by every friend, neighbor, relative, and person you know, because people have differing tastes. But it does help to lift your liqueurs into that rarified place where songs will be sung to praise them. To help achieve this level of good taste, remember that using fresh ingredients is better. When purchasing fruit, buy it as close as possible to when you'll be starting the liqueur, and buy it as ripe as possible. Always be sure to wash it before peeling or juicing. Don't let the fresh rule stop with fruit, either. Use fresh herbs and spices whenever possible. Those spices that have been hanging out in the back of the cabinet for months just won't provide the intensity of flavor that you'll want your liqueurs to possess. A reminder never hurts that you'll want to use the freshest dairy products and eggs for those sweeter mixes that feature them. It's a good idea to use fresh unsalted nuts, too. Really, following the "fresh rule" is never a bad idea, and you'll see that it leads to your liqueurs reaching the top heights in taste.

A Note on Straining

This may seem like an obvious statement, but liqueurs aren't very luscious when they're flavorless. It's the other flavorings, the herbs and spices and fruits and nuts and their fragrances, that allow us to add the descriptor "luscious" to many mixes contained here. But the flipside of using real ingredients and not artificial flavorings is that there's almost always going to be a straining step involved in making liqueurs—and usually two straining steps. And occasionally three. All this straining is why cheesecloth is essential. You may find when you've strained the recommended number of times that your liqueur is still cloudy, or still contains bits of nuts or fruits. If this is the case, strain again until it reaches the desired level of clarity. In addition, there may be instances when, a couple of days after you've bottled and the liqueur has a settled a bit, you notice that some stratification has taken place; while you thought everything was strained out, there are some floaters left in the bottles. Don't get down—just strain again. Or give the bottle a good shake before serving. This process is the downside (though really, it's not too much of a hassle) to making your own liqueurs. The upside—their amazing flavors, and the cheers and compliments you'll get when serving them—outweighs the downside by 100 to 1.

While I like using cheesecloth for straining (and a nice fine-mesh strainer for the larger pieces), you can try straining with coffee filters or muslin or other agents. I tend to find those a little too slow at times (they get clogged more easily than cheesecloth), and I think that they aren't as pure as cheesecloth—meaning they may have slight flavor of their own, altering the liqueur. Another option I've seen used is racking. Racking is basically drawing a liquid from one container to another to leave behind any sediment. To do this you have to make sure your liqueur is well settled, and you need a good-sized piece of plastic (not rubber) tubing. The method isn't too difficult. You stand up your liqueur bottle (without shaking it around) on a higher plane than the vessel you're racking into, then put the tubing into the one containing the liqueur. Making sure the tubing isn't touching any of the sediment on the bottom, you start sucking the liqueur, to start the siphoning process. Quickly put the tubing into the new container. The liquid should continue to flow downward, without the sediment. I find racking a little clumsy, but you should feel free to experiment.

KEEPING YOUR LIQUEURS

While there are recipes in this book that include specific "consume by" time frames, most don't set down a date by which the liqueurs must be drunk. This is because most liqueurs will stay good for a very long time, years even—though my guess is you'll drink them long before that much time passes. As long as you keep them sealed between servings, and don't go adding random new ingredients down the road, they'll keep well over time. They may, however, change a bit in flavor. Even after straining the flavoring agents out, the liqueurs still contain oils and other flavor essences. The overall flavor won't change dramatically (naturally, a mint flavor won't suddenly mutate to walnut), but you may find different layers of flavors emerging over time. I find that it's not a bad thing, as this deepening and changing of tastes and flavors provide even more to savor.

QUICK COCKTAIL HINTS

L iqueurs taste pretty great on their own (darn great, actually), but many in this book make fine additions to cocktails and drinks, so many of the recipes have cocktail ideas to go along with them. To take full advantage of this, it's a good idea to stock up on your bar tools as well as your liqueur-making tools. Without much hassle or shopping, you'll be ready to whip out delicious drinks in no time.

The first and most important thing you'll need is a cocktail shaker. There are two choices, the cobbler shaker and the Boston shaker. The first has a bigger bottom piece covered by a smaller top piece (which should fit together snugly to reduce any chance of spilling). The top piece usually has a built-in strainer and a cap—sometimes the cap is a handy measuring device too. Using a cobbler shaker is easy. Just put ice and ingredients in the bottom piece, secure the top piece good and tight, and shake, shake, shake. Remove the cap, strain into glasses, garnish if needed, and serve. A Boston shaker (our second type) has a glass bottom cup and a metal top cup. To use a Boston shaker, first put ice and ingredients in the bottom cup. Then carefully insert the metal top cup into the bottom cup and, using your palm, thump the bottom of the metal cup, making a seal between the two pieces. Shake holding one piece in each hand. Place the shaker on a flat surface, metal side down. Carefully tap the metal piece to break the seal. With a separate strainer, strain the drinks into glasses and serve. I think it's good prac- tice (unless specific instructions say different) to shake drinks for at least 10 to 15 seconds.

There are hosts of other bar tools that will help with your cocktail- ing. Even if your shaker comes with a measuring device, a jigger for measuring ingredients is a must (you'll always need more than one measuring device). Since some of the liqueur recipes call for fresh juice (and many drinks contain fresh juices), a handheld juice squeezer, lever-model juicer, or motorized juice extractor is a lifesaver—or at least a drink saver. Other bar tools that'll come in handy when using your liqueurs as drink ingredients include a good blender, a long stir- ring spoon, an ice bucket and ice scoop, and an assortment of chic swizzle sticks and straws. There's no need to serve up these suave and sweet liqueurs in an unstylish setting.

A GOOD GLASSWARE ADDICTION

Your liqueur *du jour* is done and strained, your peeps or a particular favorite person are on the couch or at the home bar waiting for the first sample, and you come striding in with a look of triumph—and then serve up the succulent nectar in a plastic cup. The moment drops into the mud, and the cheers ready to burst from lips turn sour. Okay, maybe it's not that drastic to serve in unattractive glasses, but after toiling on your delicious liqueur, there's no reason not to display it in an attractive glass. Actually, one of the sometimes unnoticed plusses from making your own liqueur is that you'll get to, and need to—and want to—invest in cordial and other glasses. I've found that buying the glassware itself can be quite an exciting experience. (In fact, I've found this out to such a degree that there's not an empty shelf in our glassware cabinet—and my wife just sighs when I start poking around the glass counter in antiques shops.) Liqueur or cordial glasses come in all shapes, sizes, and colors. For serving your homemade masterpieces straight up, I think a glass with a smaller bowl works best; for on-the-rocks occasions, you'll want either a fancy stemmed glass with a larger bowl (to hold the ice) or an old-fashioned or rocks glass. I suggest investing in sets of both old-fashioneds and stemmed glasses with shallow bowls, at least to start with, as well as a nice set of cocktail (martini) glasses for when you're mixing and shaking. Don't your homemade beauties deserve the best? I think they do.

THE FINAL INGREDIENTS: PATIENCE AND ENJOYMENT

All this talk about tasty liqueurs served up in lovely glasses or shaken into cocktails is enough to make the mouth water and the mind slip into a reverie of soirées and celebrations highlighted by your own creations. It's also enough to make you want to get started right now. Which brings up the last ingredient needed to make liqueurs— patience. No really good liqueurs are going to be ready in five minutes, or even overnight. The key is giving them a bit of time, so that the essences of the ingredients really mingle and come out shining bright (or subtly, in some cases). I know how hard it can be, though; as the

song says, the waiting is the hardest part. It's a necessary part, however, so no matter how antsy you're getting to strain that stuff and start
drinking, take a deep breath, step back, and know that time will pass
much more quickly than you think.

The other ingredient you'll never want to forget when making your
liqueur is enjoyment. It should be enjoyable, not a chore. Always
remember that there's a lovely light at the end of the time tunnel, and
it's the light shining through an assortment of beautiful bottles filled with
homemade liqueurs, liqueurs that will awe and delight friends, families,
and late dates, liqueurs that you'll find yourself sipping much later,
thinking, "I remember making this—what a great job I did." And that
feeling, not to mention the tasting, is a fine, fine thing. So what are you
waiting for? Turn the page, pick out a candidate that catches your
fancy, make a list, head to the store for ingredients, and get started.
Liqueur heaven is only a short time (usually about a month) away.

Cool CITRUS MIXES

T here's a certain attitude to the citrus liqueurs contained in this chapter. It may be that they sometimes contain a base liquor with a higher alcohol content, or that you have to persevere through some serious fruit-peeling to get the creation process started. Or it could be that these suave mixtures tend toward being served ice cold, and easily take the chill off a hot day. Whatever the reason, their personality rises into that rarified realm that can only be called "cool."

Blood Orange's Revenge
A Triple Sec by Any Other Name
Grapefruit Liqueur
Limoncello
Limeoncello
Mandarino
Orangnac
Oh Clementine
Satsumama

BLOOD ORANGE'S *Revenge*

Makes about 1 ¾ pints

Blood oranges are a little creepy, and make me think of famous cinematic vampires. When drinking a blood orange mixture, I sometimes ponder being a bloodsucking fiend. Which isn't a friendly thing to be, naturally. That's why this liqueur is the Blood Orange's Revenge, because it is friendly, with a sweet nature.

4 blood oranges

1 lemon

¼ teaspoon whole cloves

2 cups vodka

1½ cups Simple Syrup (page 12)

1. Wash, dry, and peel the oranges and lemon, trimming away any white pith. Put the peels in a glass container with a tight-fitting lid.

2. Using a sharp knife, remove the layer of pith from 2 of the blood oranges. (Juice the other oranges and the lemon for drinks or cooking.) Cut the trimmed oranges into pieces and add to the peels. Stir slightly with a wooden spoon to smash up the fruit.

3. Add the cloves and vodka, stir a little and seal. Place in a cool, dry spot away from sunlight. Let sit for 2 weeks, swirling occasionally.

4. Add the simple syrup, stir well, and reseal. Return to its spot. Let sit for 2 more weeks, swirling occasionally.

5. Filter the liqueur through a fine-mesh strainer into a bowl. Strain again through a double layer of cheesecloth into a pitcher or other easy-pouring vessel. Finally, strain through 2 new layers of cheesecloth into I large bottle or a number of small bottles or jars.

A NOTE: Blood oranges contain the pigment anthocyanin, which turns the flesh a dark red.

A COCKTAIL SUGGESTION: Shake 1 ounce Blood Orange's Revenge, 2 ounces gin, and ½ ounce regular orange juice with ice. Strain into a cocktail glass and call it Antidote to a Wooden Stake.

A TRIPLE SEC
by Any Other Name

Makes about 2½ pints

Triple sec is one of the most popular liqueurs, due to its rich history as a supporting player in many cocktails including the Margarita and the Sidecar, and because of the popular brands out there (such as Grand Marnier and Cointreau). The liqueur's versatile orange base is what makes it such a player. This basic recipe I modified from one on the liqueurweb.com website, a site that, as you'd expect, specializes in liqueurs.

4 or 5 medium to large oranges

½ cup water

2 cups sugar

2 cups vodka

1. Wash, dry, and peel 2 of the oranges, trimming away any white pith. Put the peels in a glass container with a tight-fitting lid.

2. Juice the oranges (I like a strong juice extractor, but any juicer will work). You want 1 cup of fresh juice.

3. Combine the sugar and water in a saucepan, stir well, and turn on the heat to medium. Slowly add the orange juice, stirring all the while. Raise the heat to medium-high and bring the mixture just to a boil. Lower the heat a bit and simmer gently for 5 minutes. Remove from the heat and cool completely.

4. Add the syrup and the vodka to the peels, stir well, and seal. Place in a cool, dry spot away from sunlight. Let the liqueur stay calm, except for occasionally swirlings, for 1 month.

5. If it's really pulpy, filter the liqueur first through a fine-mesh strainer into a bowl. Otherwise, just strain through a double layer of cheesecloth into a pitcher or other easy-pouring vessel. Strain again through 2 new layers of cheesecloth into 1 large bottle or a number of small bottles or jars.

GRAPEFRUIT *Liqueur*

Makes about 1 ³/₄ pints

Grapefruit is stern business. So stern that even adding a catchy name (Grapeorama, for instance, or G-Fav) is treading on delicate terrain. The reason is that grapefruit is a divider and not a uniter. There is hardly any middle ground between "yep, I love grapefruit" and "yep, I hate grapefruit." Keep this in mind when serving this citrus cordial (and always serve it cold). Make sure you know where their allegiances lie first.

4 yellow grapefruits

2 cups vodka

1 teaspoon whole coriander seeds

1½ cups Simple Syrup (page 12)

1. Wash, dry, and peel the grapefruits, trimming away any white pith. Put the peels in a glass container with a tight-fitting lid. Using a sharp knife, remove the layer of pith from the grapefruits. Section the grapefruits, and then cut each section in half. Add them to the peels.

2. Add the vodka and coriander, stir well, and seal. Place in a cool, dry spot away from sunlight. Let sit for 2 weeks, swirling every few days.

3. Add the simple syrup, stir well, and reseal. Return to its spot. Let sit for 2 more weeks, swirling again a couple of times.

4. Filter the liqueur through a fine-mesh strainer into a bowl. Strain again through a double layer of cheesecloth into a pitcher or other easy-pouring vessel. Finally, strain through 2 new layers of cheesecloth into 1 large bottle or a number of small bottles or jars.

A COCKTAIL SUGGESTION: Shake 1 ounce Grapefruit Liqueur, 2 ounces vodka, and ½ ounce fresh grapefruit juice with ice. Strain into a cocktail glass and call it a Fancy Greyhound.

LIMONCELLO

Makes about 3 ½ pints

L imoncello inspires the writing of songs and poems in honor of its beautiful and powerful nature. Of course, if you spend all day penning paeans to this liqueur, you won't have time to sit enjoying it on a languid early evening. Limoncello is best served chilled, so keep it in the freezer.

4 cups grain alcohol	**1.** Wash, dry, and peel the lemons, trimming away any white pith. Put the peels in a glass container with a tight-fitting lid. (Juice the leftover lemons to use in separate drinks or in cooking.)
14 lemons	
3 cups Simple Syrup (page 12)	

1. Wash, dry, and peel the lemons, trimming away any white pith. Put the peels in a glass container with a tight-fitting lid. (Juice the leftover lemons to use in separate drinks or in cooking.)
2. Add the grain alcohol and seal. Place in a cool, dry spot away from sunlight. Let sit for 2 weeks.
3. Add the simple syrup, stir, and reseal. Return to its spot. Let sit for 2 more weeks.
4. Strain the liqueur through a double layer of cheesecloth into a pitcher or other easy-pouring vessel. Strain again through 2 new layers of cheesecloth into 1 large bottle or a number of small bottles or jars.

A NOTE: If you live in a state where grain alcohol is not readily available, you can substitute high-proof vodka here.

A COCKTAIL SUGGESTION: While Limoncello is great alone, it also is a key ingredient in the Princess, a drink my wife created. Fill a Collins glass three-quarters full with ice cubes. Add 1 ½ ounces Limoncello. Fill to about ½ inch from the top with chilled club soda. Add 5 or 6 fresh raspberries, and stir well.

LIMEONCELLO
Makes about 2¼ pints

You put the lime in the container, shake it all up, you put the vodka in the container, shake it all up, you say doctor, is there nothing I can take, you say doctor, that's as good as this lime-y drink? Okay, that's pushing the boundaries of song-modifying, but Harry Nilsson, I think, would be okay with it. And that island-y rhythm matches the island-y nature of this cordial.

7 limes	**1.** Wash, dry, and peel the limes and lemon, trimming away any white pith. Put the peels in a glass container with a tight-fitting lid. (Juice the leftover limes and lemon to use in separate drinks.)
1 lemon	
3 cups white rum	
1½ cups Simple Syrup (page 12)	**2.** Add the rum and seal. Place in a cool, dry spot away from sunlight. Let sit for 2 weeks, swirling once or twice a week.
	3. Add the simple syrup, stir, and reseal. Return to its spot. Let sit for 2 more weeks, swirling occasionally.
	4. Strain the liqueur through a double layer of cheesecloth into a pitcher or other easy-pouring vessel. Strain again through 2 new layers of cheesecloth into 1 large bottle or a number of small bottles or jars.

TWO SERVING SUGGESTIONS: I think Limeoncello is best served chilled, so store it in the freezer (or in a pinch, shake well with ice and strain into a glass). It is also tasty mixed with a little coconut syrup or cream of coconut and served over shaved ice.

A QUOTE: "'I made her a present,' he wrote, 'of a match-coat and a bottle of rum, which latter was thought much the best present of the two.'"
—Jean Jules Jusserand, *With Americans of Past and Present Days*

MANDARINO

Makes 2 pints

Thisis a simple citrus liqueur using sweet mandarin oranges to create a cordial that fits well into that intimate after-dinner-drink category. Mandarino is best served chilled, either straight from the freezer or shaken or stirred over ice.

6 mandarin oranges	**1.** Wash, dry, and peel the oranges and half of the lemon, trimming away any white pith. If the mandarin peels slip right off, scrape the inner side of the peel to remove the pith. Put the peels in a glass container with a tight-fitting lid. (Use the leftover fruit for juicing, cooking, or just eating.)
1 lemon	
2 cups vodka	
2 cups Simple Syrup (page 12)	

1. Wash, dry, and peel the oranges and half of the lemon, trimming away any white pith. If the mandarin peels slip right off, scrape the inner side of the peel to remove the pith. Put the peels in a glass container with a tight-fitting lid. (Use the leftover fruit for juicing, cooking, or just eating.)

2. Add the vodka, stir a little, and seal. Place the container in a cool, dry spot away from sunlight. Let it relax for 2 weeks, swirling every 3 or 4 days.

3. Add the simple syrup, stir well, and reseal. Return to its spot. Let sit for 2 more weeks, stopping by to swirl every 3 or 4 days.

4. Strain the liqueur through a double layer of cheesecloth into a pitcher or other easy-pouring vessel. Strain again through 2 new layers of cheesecloth into 1 large bottle or a number of small bottles or jars.

TWO COCKTAIL SUGGESTIONS: Substitute Mandarino for orange curaçao in a Chocolate Heaven (2 ounces chocolate vodka, 1 ounce Mandarino, and orange mint for garnish). Or use it instead of gin in the classic Alexander (1 ounce Mandarino, 1 ounce crème de cacao, and 1 ounce heavy cream, shaken with ice and strained into a cocktail glass). The latter I'd call an Alexarino or a Mandarander, but maybe that's just me.

ORANGNAC

Makes about 1 ½ pints

The base alcohol here is Cognac, which has a silver-spoon reputation. But you must leave pecuniary considerations at the door on this occasion. You don't want to miss out on this tempting orange beauty, and once you go shopping, you'll realize that Cognacs aren't overly expensive. Of course, when serving Orangnac, there's no need to spread this financial fact around. It's fun to be thought a high roller, after all.

½ cup freshly grated orange zest (from 3 to 4 oranges)

2 tablespoons water

¾ cup sugar

2½ cups Cognac

1. Put the orange zest, water, and sugar in a large bowl. Using a muddler or wooden spoon, mash everything together. This may take some work, but keep mashing until the sugar and water are well combined into the zest, making a sugary orange ooze.

2. Put the mixture in a glass container with a tight-fitting lid. Add the Cognac, swirl or stir slightly, and seal. Place in a cool, dry spot away from sunlight. Let sit for 2 months, swirling twice a week.

3. Strain the liqueur through a double layer of cheesecloth into a pitcher or other easy-pouring vessel. Strain again through 2 new layers of cheesecloth into 1 large bottle or a number of small bottles or jars, and reseal. Let sit for another 2 weeks before serving.

A NOTE: It's best to zest over the bowl to capture any extra orange oils that burst out during the zesting process.

A SERVING SUGGESTION: This is a nice after-dinner drink, served neat in a snifter or over ice in an old-fashioned glass.

A QUOTE: "We will spend thy money there or at the theatre, or we will treat her to French wine or Cognac in the Aurelius Garden."
—William Makepeace Thackeray, *Vanity Fair*

Oh CLEMENTINE

Makes about 2 ¼ pints

C lementines the fruit aren't sad at all, unlike the folksy ballad about a miner's dying daughter. Instead, they're a medium-size member of the mandarin orange family, usually seedless, slightly sweet, and sometimes called the "Christmas orange" or the "Algerian tangerine." They are generally available in wooden crates in the market from late summer past Christmas.

5 clementines

10 mint leaves

3 cups vodka

1½ cups Simple Syrup (page 12)

1 teaspoon pure vanilla extract

1. Wash, dry, and peel the clementines, trimming away any white pith. If the peels slip right off, scrape the inner side of the peel to remove the pith. Put the peels and the mint leaves in a glass container with a tight-fitting lid. Using a muddler or wooden spoon gently muddle the mint leaves and peels until the leaves are slightly mashed.

2. Add the vodka, stir, and seal. Place in a cool, dry spot away from sunlight. Let sit for 2 weeks, stopping to say "howdy" and swirl a couple of times a week.

3. Add the simple syrup and vanilla, stir well, and reseal. Return to its spot and let sit for 2 more weeks, swirling a couple of times a week.

4. Strain the liqueur through a double layer of cheesecloth into a pitcher or other easy-pouring vessel. Strain again through 2 new layers of cheesecloth into 1 large bottle or a number of small bottles or jars.

A COCKTAIL SUGGESTION: I like this best served solo and ice cold, but it also plays well with ginger ale over ice in a highball glass.

SATSUMAMA

Makes about 1³/₄ pints

Afavorite in Japan (where they have been cultivated for 700 or so years), the satsuma orange is beloved for its sweet taste with a hint of tang. Because the peel comes off so easily, it's tempting when making this treat to just chuck the whole skin in there, without removing the pith—but don't do it, because the pith will ruin the taste.

5 satsuma oranges

½ teaspoon whole anise seeds

½ teaspoon whole cloves

2 cups brandy

1 cup honey

1. Wash, dry, and peel the satsumas, trimming away any white pith. If the peels slip right off, scrape the inner side of the peel to remove the pith. Put the peels in a glass container with a tight-fitting lid.

2. Juice 2 of the satsumas; you want ½ cup juice. (Use the others for snacks or more juicing.) Add the juice, the anise seeds, cloves, and brandy to the peels. Stir well and seal. Place in a cool, dry spot away from sunlight. Let sit for 2 weeks, swirling occasionally.

3. Add the honey, stir well, and reseal. Return to its spot. Let sit for 3 weeks more, but open once a week to stir, and swirl occasionally between the stirring times.

4. Filter the liqueur through a fine-mesh strainer into a bowl. Strain again through a double layer of cheesecloth into a pitcher or other easy-pouring vessel. Finally, strain through 2 new layers of cheesecloth into 1 large bottle or a number of small bottles or jars.

A COCKTAIL SUGGESTION: Shake 1 ounce Satsumama and 2 ounces brandy or Cognac with ice. Strain into a cocktail glass and call it a Satsumacar.

A *Fiesta of* FRUIT FLAVORS

I'm not saying that when you step into the fiesta and start serving up the liqueurs in this chapter, you must sing "La Cucaracha" and dance around a large, colorful hat. But at least put on a stylin' celebratory grin, knowing that you're taking advantage of some of the best of nature's fruity bounty, because you'll find a whole cornucopia of fruit contained in the following pages: raspberries, bananas, blueberries, pears, and many of their fruity brethren.

Always Bet on Blackberries
Applicious
Fruit Basket Mix-Up
A Fair Pear
Banana Beauty
Righteous Raspberry
Pineapple Pride
Feeling Peachy
Very Cherry
Singing the Blueberries
Strawberry Gold

Always Bet on
BLACKBERRIES

Makes about 3¼ pints

I f I were going to place a bet, it would be on one of two things. First, on the fact that by using fresh blackberries here, especially those you've picked, you'll end up with a more scrumptious result. And second, on how delicious desserts, even simple ice cream, can become with a little of this drizzled over the top.

3 cups fresh blackberries

1 lemon

3 cups vodka

3 cups Simple Syrup (page 12)

1. Gently wash the blackberries and dry on towels. When completely dry, put them in a glass container with a tight-fitting lid. Wash, dry, and peel the lemon, trimming away any white pith. (Use the lemon as you will.) Add the lemon peel to the blackberries. Using a muddler or wooden spoon, muddle the blackberries and peel. You want them to be a little mushed, so don't be shy.

2. Add the vodka, stir, and seal. Place in a cool, dry spot away from sunlight. Let sit for 2 weeks, swirling occasionally.

3. Add the simple syrup, stir again, and reseal. Return to its spot. Let sit for 2 more weeks.

4. Strain the liqueur through a double layer of cheesecloth into a pitcher or other easy-pouring vessel. Strain again through 2 new layers of cheesecloth into 1 large bottle or a number of small bottles or jars.

A SERVING SUGGESTION: This is dandy chilled, but also fine at room temperature, especially if serving over ice cream or a pie or tart.

A COCKTAIL SUGGESTION: Shake 1 ounce of this, 2 ounces vodka, and 1 ounce Chambord with ice. Strain into a cocktail glass and garnish with a lemon twist. Call it The Right Bet.

APPLICIOUS

Makes about 1¾ pints

I f I were to suggest that you travel around the country introducing Applicious to people from Maine to southern Cal, would that sound weird, or would it sound like the beginning of a folk legend? I, and Johnny Appleseed (who would be proud), think the latter. I suggest going with an apple variety that boasts a little of the tart, such as Granny Smith; if you tend toward a sweeter direction, then try Gala.

5 apples

1 lemon

2 cups vodka

1½ cups Simple Syrup (page 12)

1. Core and coarsely chop the apples. Wash, dry, and peel the lemon, trimming away any white pith. Put the apples and lemon peel in a glass container with a tight-fitting lid. (Juice the leftover lemon to use in cooking.)

2. Add the vodka, stir and seal. Place in a cool, dry spot away from sunlight. Let sit for 2 weeks, swirling once or twice a week.

3. Add the simple syrup, stir, and reseal. Return to its spot. Let sit for 2 more weeks, swirling occasionally.

4. Filter the liqueur through a fine-mesh strainer into a bowl. Strain again through a double layer of cheesecloth into a pitcher or other easy-pouring vessel. Finally, strain through 2 new layers of cheesecloth into another pitcher or bottle. Check that the liqueur is free of debris. If it isn't, repeat this step until the desired clarity is reached. Pour the liqueur into 1 large bottle or a number of small bottles or jars, and let the legend begin.

A COCKTAIL SUGGESTION: Shake 1½ ounces Applicious and 2 ounces vodka with ice. Strain into a cocktail glass. Garnish your Applicious Appletini with a lemon twist or apple slice.

A QUOTE: "Lo! sweeten'd with the summer light, / The full-juiced apple, waxing over-mellow, / Drops in a silent autumn night."
—Alfred, Lord Tennyson, "Song of the Lotus-Eaters"

FRUIT BASKET *Mix-Up*

Makes about 3½ pints

I don't know that it's safe to play the children's game of the same name when drinking this liqueur. (The game is played with a group of kids sitting in a circle on chairs, with one kid standing in the middle. Each kid is assigned a fruit name. The one in the middle calls out a fruit, and everyone with that designation jumps up to find a new chair. The kid in the middle will also be looking for a chair, leaving another kid to become "it" in the middle.) However, you could promise a bottle of this as a gift to the parents of the winner.

2 limes

4 lemons

4 oranges

2 tangerines

2 satsumas or clementines

4 cups high-proof vodka or grain alcohol

3 cups Simple Syrup (page 12)

1. Ask a good friend over (or call your spouse into the room with a smile). Together, wash, dry, and peel the fruits, trimming away any white pith. Put the peels in a glass container with a tight-fitting lid. (Juice or reserve the leftover fruit for another use.)

2. Add the vodka, stir slightly, and seal. Place in a cool, dry spot away from sunlight. Let sit for 2 weeks, swirling occasionally.

3. Add the simple syrup, stir well, and reseal. Return to its spot. Let sit for 2 more weeks, swirling again a couple of times.

4. Strain the liqueur through a double layer of cheesecloth into a pitcher or other easy-pouring vessel. Strain again through 2 new layers of cheesecloth into 1 large bottle or a number of small bottles or jars.

A NOTE: This is a pretty scrumptious fruity mix, but only reaches those heights when chilled. Act accordingly.

A COCKTAIL SUGGESTION: Serve 2 ounces in a highball glass over crushed ice, topped with club soda and garnished with either a lemon or lime twist.

A Fair PEAR

Makes about 2¼ pints

Don't imagine that the "fair" in this tickler's title means "middling." On the contrary, it should be thought of as a carnival reference, because this luscious mix is as much fun as the midway. When consuming it, feel free to sing "I went to the Fair Pear, the birds and the beasts drank there, the big baboon by the light of the moon, was sipping his potion of pear."

5 Bartlett pears (or your favorite variety)

½ of a washed and dried lemon

3 cups vodka

1½ cups Simple Syrup (page 12)

1. Core and coarsely chop the pears. Peel the lemon, trimming away any white pith. Put the pears and lemon peel in a glass container with a tight-fitting lid. (Juice the leftover lemon to use in lemonade.)

2. Add the vodka, stir, and seal. Place in a cool, dry spot away from sunlight. Let sit for 2 weeks, spinning the container carefully twice a week.

3. Add the simple syrup, stir well, and reseal. Return to its spot. Let sit for 2 more weeks, spinning carefully twice a week.

4. Filter the liqueur through a fine-mesh strainer into a bowl. Strain again through a double layer of cheesecloth into a pitcher or other easy-pouring vessel. Finally, strain through 2 new layers of cheesecloth into another pitcher or bottle. Check that the liqueur is free of debris. If it isn't, repeat this step until the desired clarity is reached. Pour the liqueur into 1 large bottle or a number of small bottles or jars.

A COCKTAIL SUGGESTION: Serve over ice mixed with 7UP or club soda. It's also dandy solo—just be sure it's chilled.

BANANA *Beauty*

Makes about 2 ½ pints

I'm Banana Beauty and I've come to say, banana liqueur must be made a certain way. When it sits just long enough in a container sealed snug, you'll have a treat that you'll want to chug. The creation of this cordial involves a little studied persistence, because you want to make sure all the banana bits get filtered out at the end.

2 medium to large bananas

4 cups vodka

1½ cups Simple Syrup (page 12)

1 tablespoon pure vanilla extract

1. Peel the bananas and put them in a glass container with a tight-fitting lid. Add the vodka. Using a wooden spoon, mash up the bananas a bit. Seal and place in a cool, dry spot away from sunlight. Let sit for 2 weeks.

2. Add the simple syrup, stir briefly, and reseal. Return to its spot. Let sit for 2 more weeks, swirling once a week.

3. Add the vanilla, stir briefly with your trusty wooden spoon, and reseal. Return it to its spot yet again. Let sit for 1 more week.

4. Filter the liquid through a fine-mesh strainer into a bowl (the banana pieces will look gnarly). Carefully strain through a double layer of cheesecloth into a pitcher or other easy-pouring vessel. Finally, strain through 2 new layers of cheesecloth into another pitcher or bottle. Check that the liqueur is free of debris. If it isn't, repeat this step until the desired clarity is reached. Pour the liqueur into 1 large bottle or a number of small bottles or jars.

5. After a day or two, you may notice that a bit of sediment has settled in the bottom of the bottle or bottles. You can just shake it up before each use, or you can pour off the clear liqueur into new bottles. Don't toss the sediment—mix it up with ice cream. Yummy.

A COCKTAIL SUGGESTION: To make a Chocolate-Covered Banana, shake 1 ounce Banana Beauty, 1 ounce chocolate vodka, and 1 ounce crème de cacao with ice. Strain the mixture into a cocktail glass.

Righteous RASPBERRY

Makes about 2 quarts

I t's not required that you pick your own raspberries from a patch
that you grew from seeds in your backyard for this berry-licious
liqueur to come together. It is required that you use fresh raspberries, as frozen don't have the same tangy-sweet flavor.

**4 cups fresh
raspberries**

4 cups vodka

**¼ cup freshly
squeezed lemon
juice**

**4 cups Simple
Syrup (page 12)**

1. Gently wash the raspberries and dry on
towels. Once completely dry, put them in a glass
container with a tight-fitting lid.

2. Add the vodka and lemon juice and seal.
Place in a cool, dry spot away from sunlight.
Let sit for 1 week.

3. Swirl for about 2 seconds. Let sit for 1
more week.

4. Add the simple syrup, stir with a wooden
spoon, and reseal. Return to its spot. Let sit for
2 more weeks.

5. Strain the liqueur through a double layer
of cheesecloth into a pitcher or other easy-
pouring vessel. Strain again through 2 new
layers of cheesecloth into 1 large bottle or a
number of small bottles or jars.

A COCKTAIL SUGGESTION: This liqueur is fine by itself, served
chilled or over ice, but it also makes a great addition to Champagne. Just put
1 ounce in a flute and fill to the rim with bubbly. It'll be a brunch hit.

PINEAPPLE *Pride*

Makes about 2 ¼ pints

I suppose you could use canned pineapple chunks and juice here instead of fresh, but then you wouldn't be able to take as much pride in it, would you? Take the plunge and use the fresh pineapple, and be filled with pride. This liqueur tastes best after chilling.

1 medium-size
pineapple

2 teaspoons freshly
squeezed lemon
juice

3 cups white rum

1½ cups Simple
Syrup (page 12)

1. Slice the top and bottom off the pineapple. Carefully trim away all of the skin and the eyes. Core and chop the pineapple, reserving any juice. Put 2 cups of the pineapple chunks and I tablespoon of the juice in a glass container with a tight-fitting lid. Using a muddler or wooden spoon, muddle the pineapple chunks until they're slightly broken up.

2. Add the lemon juice and rum. Stir well and seal. Place in a cool, dry spot away from sunlight. Let sit for 2 weeks, swirling occasionally.

3. Add the simple syrup, stir again, and reseal. Return to its spot. Let sit for 2 more weeks, swirling occasionally.

4. Filter the liqueur through a fine-mesh strainer into a bowl. Strain again through a double layer of cheesecloth into a pitcher or other easy-pouring vessel. Finally, strain through 2 new layers of cheesecloth into I large bottle or a number of small bottles or jars.

TWO COCKTAIL SUGGESTIONS: Blend 2 ounces of this with 1 ounce cream of coconut, 2 ounces dark rum, 1 cup ice, and 1 ounce heavy cream to make a tasty variation on the Piña Colada. Or just mix it with a little dark rum and ice in a cocktail shaker and strain into a cocktail glass.

Feeling PEACHY

Makes 1¾ pints

P each liqueur gets a bad rap. Too often representatives of the genre are so overly saccharine that they should be on every dentist's top 10 list of items to stay away from. The peach, though, is such a subtle fruit that I think the liqueur should match it, and so here the sugar is subservient to its flavor.

4 peaches

½ of a washed and dried lemon

2 cups vodka

1½ cups Simple Syrup (page 12)

1. Using a sharp knife, split the peaches open, remove the pits (reserve them for Amande, page 50, if you want), and coarsely chop the peaches. You should have approximately 2½ cups. Put them in a glass container with a tight-fitting lid.

2. Peel the lemon, trimming away any white pith. Add the lemon peel to the peaches. (Use the lemon as you will.)

3. Add the vodka, stir well, and seal. Place in a cool, dry spot away from sunlight. Let sit for 2 weeks, stopping by to swirl the container every couple of days.

4. Add the simple syrup, stir well, and reseal. Return to its spot. Let sit for 2 more weeks, again swirling the container every few days.

5. Filter the liqueur through a fine-mesh strainer into a bowl. Strain again through a double layer of cheesecloth into a pitcher or other easy-pouring vessel. Finally, strain through 2 new layers of cheesecloth into another pitcher or bottle. Check that the liqueur is free of debris. If it isn't, repeat this step until the desired clarity is reached. Pour the liqueur into 1 large bottle or a number of small bottles or jars.

A COCKTAIL SUGGESTION: To make a dandy Fuzzy Navel, combine 2 ounces Feeling Peachy, 1 ounce vodka, and 2 ounces fresh orange juice in a cocktail shaker with ice. Shake, strain into a highball glass half-full with ice, and garnish with a peach slice.

Very **CHERRY**

Makes about 2 ¼ pints

Picking your own cherries is optional when making this popular cherry liqueur, but if it's possible, I suggest it. Being involved with the fruit from the beginning is extra rewarding. I call this Very Cherry because it uses what I think is the cherry king, the Rainier, renowned for its amazing flavor. If you can't wrangle Rainiers, other cherries are okay, too.

3½ cups Rainier cherries

1½ cups vodka

1½ cups brandy

1½ cups Simple Syrup (page 12)

1. Remove the cherry stems. Using a paring knife, slice each cherry from top to bottom and then back to the top again (slicing around the whole cherry) to expose the pits. Put the cherries in a glass container with a tight-fitting lid.

2. Add the vodka and brandy, stir slightly, and seal. Place in a cool, dry spot away from sunlight. Let sit for 2 weeks, twirling the container every other day in a careful manner.

3. Add the simple syrup, stir well, and reseal. Return to its spot. Let sit for 2 more weeks, following the same twirling schedule as in step 2.

4. Filter the liqueur through a fine-mesh strainer into a bowl. Strain again through a double layer of cheesecloth into a pitcher or other easy-pouring vessel. Finally, strain through 2 new layers of cheesecloth into 1 large bottle or a number of small bottles or jars. Let sit for 1 more week before partaking.

A SERVING SUGGESTION: Serve Very Cherry on its own, chilled, or pour a little over a crisp or a brown betty.

A QUOTE: "Why, Mr. Mannering, people must have brandy and tea, and there's none in the country but what comes this way—and then there's short accounts, and maybe a keg or two, or a dozen pounds left at your stable door."
—Sir Walter Scott, *Guy Mannering*

Singing the BLUEBERRIES

Makes about 2¾ pints

I t's easy to sing a bluesy song when drinking Singing the Blueberries. It doesn't have to be a depressing bluesy song, though (I like to avoid the depressing when singing about liqueurs). Even though most blues songs are a little on the down side, it's okay, when singing of this liqueur, to keep the slower pace and 12-bar structure while changing the lyrics to reflect your liqueur love.

3 cups fresh blueberries

½ of a washed and dried lemon

3 cups vodka

2½ cups Simple Syrup (page 12)

1. Gently wash the blueberries and dry on towels. Once completely dry, put them in a glass container with a tight-fitting lid. Peel the lemon, trimming away any white pith. Add the lemon peel to the blueberries. (Use the lemon as you will.) Using a muddler or wooden spoon, muddle the fruit and peel well.

2. Add the vodka, stir smoothly, and seal. Place in a cool, dry spot away from sunlight. Let sit for 2 weeks, shaking it up occasionally.

3. Add the simple syrup, stir again, and reseal. Return to its spot. Let sit for 2 more weeks.

4. Strain the liqueur through a double layer of cheesecloth into a pitcher or other easy-pouring vessel. Strain again through 2 new layers of cheesecloth into I large bottle or a number of small bottles or jars.

A COCKTAIL SUGGESTION: Pour 1½ ounces chilled Singing the Blueberries in a flute and top with chilled Champagne. That'll remove any amount of blue feeling.

STRAWBERRY *Gold*

Makes about 2 pints

T his doesn't mean you're actually going to turn strawberries into gold, just create a drink that's precious like gold. After all, if you say you can turn strawberries into gold, the king will hear you and lock you in a tower until you do it. Then you'll have to contact Rumpelstiltskin, who will extract some seriously troublesome promises from you.

3½ cups fresh strawberries

3 cups vodka

1½ cups Simple Syrup (page 12)

1½ teaspoons pure vanilla extract

1. Gently wash the strawberries and dry on towels. When completely dry, remove the stems (I cut off the tops of the strawberries, because the flesh around the stems is not as sweet as the rest of the berry) and any blemished spots. Coarsely chop the strawberries (you should have 3 ½ cups). Put them in a glass container with a tight-fitting lid.

2. Add the vodka, stir well, and seal. Place in a dry, cool spot away from sunlight. Let sit for 2 weeks, whirling the strawberries around the jar every 3 days.

3. Add the simple syrup and vanilla, stir, and reseal. Return to its spot. Let sit for 2 more weeks, whirling the contents every other day.

4. Filter the liqueur through a fine-mesh strainer into a bowl. Strain again through a double layer of cheesecloth into a pitcher or other easy-pouring vessel. Finally, strain through 2 new layers of cheesecloth into 1 large bottle or a number of small bottles or jars.

A COCKTAIL SUGGESTION: Shake 2 ounces Strawberry Gold, 2 ounces vodka, and 1 ounce simple syrup with ice. Strain into a sugar-rimmed cocktail glass. This works with Singing the Blueberries (left), too.

A QUOTE: "About nice drinks, anyhow, my recollection of the 'cobblers' (with strawberries and snow on top of the large tumblers), and also the exquisite wines, and the perfect and mild French brandy, help the regretful reminiscence."
—Walt Whitman, *Prose Works*

NUTTY AND SPICY *Necessities*

The long and intricate history of liqueurs made with an assortment of spices and nuts traces its way across multiple continents, making stops to pick up whatever's desired to craft blends boasting layer upon layer of flavors. Don't let this history make you think that these liqueurs are going to be pompous and show up at the party in sport coats, though—they're necessities because they arrive ready for a good time, adding a little joyous nuttiness to any occasion.

Amande
Nocino
Basil Grappa
Anisetter
Spiced Rum
Cinnamon Snap
Ginger Ice
The Hot Horse
Heroic Hazelnut
Millefiori
Minty Fresh

AMANDE

Makes about 1 ½ pints

Not to get too Continental here, but *amande* is French for "almond." This simple-yet-subtle infusion is just almonds, vodka, and simple syrup. And peach pits (which, interestingly, taste almond-y). Almonds are actually related to peaches and other stone fruits, and this kinship means that a little of this liqueur drizzled over a peach cobbler is sweet magic. Or, if you prefer, *magie douce*. It's also lovely served solo, chilled or at room temperature.

½ cup skin-on raw almonds, chopped	**1.** Put the almonds, peach pits, and vodka in a glass container with a tight-fitting lid. Stir and seal. Place in a cool, dry spot away from sunlight. Let sit for 2 weeks, swirling occasionally.
4 whole peach pits, slightly crushed	
2 cups vodka	**2.** Add the simple syrup, stir again, and reseal. Return to its spot and let sit for 2 more weeks.
1 cup Simple Syrup (page 12)	**3.** Strain the liqueur through a double layer of cheesecloth into a pitcher or other easy-pouring vessel. Strain again through 2 new layers of cheesecloth into another pitcher or bottle. Check that the liqueur is free of almond bits. If it isn't, repeat this step until it is. Pour the liqueur into 1 large bottle or a number of small bottles or jars.

A NOTE: Be sure to buy whole almonds, and chop them right before adding them to the vodka. The chopping releases the essential oils that bring out the desired almond flavor.

A QUOTE: "His gentle, soothing words and smiles were as soothing and softening as almond oil. And Anna soon felt this."

—Leo Tolstoy, *Anna Karenina*

NOCINO

Makes 3 ¼ pints

This is a variation on an Italian liqueur that uses walnuts. Walnuts may not be seen in the same glamorous light as hazelnuts or pistachios, but they provide a wonderfully sturdy base flavor here, and deserve to get a curtain call. Because of the richness and thickness of this liqueur, it'll take the edge off a cool morning (okay, in coffee). However, it also goes well with a spring afternoon. Now you see why walnuts deserve that curtain call—it's their versatility.

2 cups walnuts, coarsely chopped

½ teaspoon whole cloves

4 cups vodka

1 teaspoon pure vanilla extract

2½ cups Simple Syrup (page 12)

1. Combine the walnuts, cloves, and vodka in a glass container with a tight-fitting lid. Stir well and seal. Place in a cool, dry spot away from sunlight. Let sit for 2 weeks, shaking occasionally.

2. Add the vanilla and simple syrup, stir, and reseal. Return to its spot. Let sit for 2 more weeks.

3. Strain the liqueur through a double layer of cheesecloth into a pitcher or other easy-pouring vessel. Strain again through 2 new layers of cheesecloth into another pitcher or bottle. If it's still cloudy, repeat this step until it's clear. Pour the liqueur into 1 large bottle or a number of small bottles or jars. It's best if you can let this sit for 2 more weeks before serving, to really let the walnut flavor combine with the spices.

A COCKTAIL SUGGESTION: Nocino can take the place of any nutty/spicy liqueur, such as amaretto or Frangelico, in a cocktail. For example, try a little of it mixed with bourbon and orange juice, and taste the way the flavors combine without overwhelming.

Basil GRAPPA
Makes about 1 ³/₄ pints

Most won't jump right into the idea of infusing grappa—because most, or at least many, are a tad scared of grappa. I can understand this, having been nervous the first time I tried it (and I like bitter—and biting—drinks on occasion). I was even more nervous the second time, because my first grappa had a bit of the taste of gasoline. But the second time it was more what I've come to expect with grappa: a serious nature and rewarding flavor. If you haven't come around yet to enjoying grappa straight, this softer version may be right up your after-dinner-drink alley.

1 cup loosely packed fresh basil leaves

1 tablespoon freshly squeezed lemon juice

3 cups grappa

½ cup Simple Syrup (page 12)

1. Put the basil and lemon juice in a glass container with a tight-fitting lid. Using a muddler or wooden spoon, muddle the basil leaves and lemon juice.

2. Add the grappa, stir, and seal. Place the container in a cool, dry spot away from sunlight. Let sit for 1 week, swirling occasionally.

3. Add the simple syrup, stir, and reseal. Return to its spot. Let sit for 2 more weeks, swirling occasionally.

4. Strain the liqueur through a double layer of cheesecloth into a pitcher or other easy-pouring vessel. Strain again through 2 new layers of cheesecloth into 1 large bottle or a number of small bottles or jars.

A SERVING SUGGESTION: Serve Basil Grappa chilled or at room temperature in small glasses; it's especially good for alleviating that over-full feeling when you've had a couple bites too many.

ANISETTER

Makes about 1 ½ pints

N ot a sloppy large red dog, but a liqueur that echoes some of the absinthe substitutes such as Herbsaint and Pernod, with a little more sweetness. Like those cordials, Anisetter doesn't contain any wormwood or other potentially brain-jangling ingredients. It does take a little work to make, though. Persevere (or buy an electric spice grinder) and you'll be rewarded, because this is dreamy served over ice.

1 tablespoon whole anise seeds

1 teaspoon whole coriander seeds

2 cups vodka

1 cup Simple Syrup (page 12)

1. Using a mortar and pestle, crush the anise and coriander seeds. Put them in a glass container with a tight-fitting lid.

2. Add the vodka, stir a couple of times with a wooden spoon, and seal. Place in a cool, dry spot away from sunlight for 2 weeks.

3. Add the simple syrup, stir a few more times, and reseal. Return to its spot. Let sit for 2 more weeks, swirling once or twice a week.

4. Filter the liqueur through a fine-mesh strainer into a bowl. Carefully strain through a double layer of cheesecloth into a pitcher or other easy-pouring vessel. Finally, strain through 2 new layers of cheesecloth into another pitcher or bottle. Check that the liqueur is free of debris. If it isn't, repeat this step until the desired clarity is reached. Pour the liqueur into 1 large bottle or a number of small bottles or jars. Let sit for 1 more week before serving.

A COCKTAIL SUGGESTION: Shake 1½ ounces Anisetter with 1½ ounces gin and ½ ounce grenadine in an ice-filled cocktail shaker, and strain into a cocktail glass. You'll be walking into a variation of an Asylum—but of your own free will.

A QUOTE: "Don Pedro—who rose with the dawn and had a busy time of it during the day—when he had finished his after-dinner cigar and taken his cup of coffee and his glass of anisette, felt fatigued, and went, according to his custom, to take a long nap."

—Juan Valera, *Pepita Jiménez* (David Rowland, translator)

Spiced **RUM**
Makes 1 ³/₄ to 2 pints

Unlike the summery Caribbean Queen (page 68), this rum liqueur warms up as well as it plays the typical tropical beat. I like it best when it's a little chillier outside, when the snow is rising. It would make an ideal filler for the St. Bernard's barrel (the small one around its collar). Or, you could just make yourself a little belt to mirror the dog's, fill yours with Spiced Rum, and never leave the lodge.

¾ teaspoon ground cinnamon

½ teaspoon whole cloves

¾ teaspoon ground nutmeg

½ teaspoon whole coriander seeds

¾ teaspoon minced peeled fresh ginger

3 cups white rum

¾ cup Simple Syrup (page 12)

1 teaspoon pure vanilla extract

1. Put the cinnamon, cloves, nutmeg, coriander, ginger, and rum in a glass container with a tight-fitting lid. Stir briefly, seal, and place in a cool, dry spot away from any lingering winter sun. Let sit for 2 weeks, shaking occasionally to keep it from hibernating.

2. Add the simple syrup and vanilla, stir briefly, and reseal. Return to its spot. Let sit for 3 more long, cold weeks, swirling every few days.

3. Strain the liqueur through a double layer of cheesecloth into a pitcher or other easy-pouring vessel. Strain again through 2 new layers of cheesecloth into 1 large bottle or a number of small bottles or jars.

A COCKTAIL SUGGESTION: If it's really been a long winter, shake 1½ ounces of Spiced Rum, ½ ounce Pernod, ½ ounce crème de noyaux, ½ ounce orange curaçao, and 1 egg yolk with ice. You'll be swilling an Eye-Opener and will wake right up. (Remember, because this cocktail contains raw egg, don't serve it to anyone with a compromised immune system.)

CINNAMON *Snap*

Makes about 2 pints

S nap, snap, snap. It's like a bad parody of Beat poets once this liqueur is served, as no one desires to actually speak (as it involves not sipping for a minute), and so everyone is reduced to snapping their appreciation. Really, though, is any sort of adulation a bad thing?

1 tablespoon minced peeled fresh ginger

1 teaspoon ground cinnamon

3 cups vodka

1 cup Simple Syrup (page 12)

1. Put the ginger, cinnamon, and vodka in a glass container with a tight-fitting lid. Seal and place in a cool, dry spot away from sunlight. Let sit for I week.

2. Swirl the container for about 5 seconds. Return to its spot and let sit for 2 more weeks, swirling it for 5 seconds every 3 or 4 days.

3. Add the simple syrup, reseal, and swirl for 5 seconds. Return again to its spot. Let sit for 2 more weeks, swirling for 5 seconds every 3 or 4 days.

4. Filter the liqueur through a double layer of cheesecloth into a bowl. Strain again through another double layer of cheesecloth into a pitcher or other easy-pouring vessel. Finally, strain through 2 new layers of cheesecloth into I large bottle or a number of small bottles or jars.

A SERVING SUGGESTION: This cinnamon treat is especially good over vanilla ice cream, if you're in need of a little spicy dessert. It also goes well as a sipped accompaniment to ice cream, if you're opposed to combining the two right in the bowl.

A QUOTE: "While he from forth the closet brought a heap / Of candied apple, quince, and plum, and gourd; / With jellies soother than the creamy curd, / And lucent syrops, tinct with cinnamon"

—John Keats, "The Eve of St. Agnes"

GINGER *Ice*

Makes about 2 1/2 pints

From inside, a really icy day is a pretty picture, with crystals forming along tree branches and other objects to the point where everything looks like sparkling jewelry. However, when you're walking out into that cold, it often loses its luster. In somewhat the same way, Ginger Ice, which tastes crisp and clear, loses some luster if not consumed directly from the freezer, or at least well shaken with ice. This cordial is a chilly charmer with the added bonus of warming you once it settles in, a quality those icicles can't claim.

2 tablespoons minced peeled fresh ginger

3 cups vodka

1½ cups Simple Syrup (page 12)

1. Put the ginger and vodka in a glass container with a tight-fitting lid. Stir well, seal, and place in a cool, dry spot away from sunlight. Let sit for 2 weeks, shaking occasionally.

2. Add the simple syrup, stir, and reseal. Return to its spot. Let sit for 2 more weeks.

3. Strain the liqueur through a double layer of cheesecloth into a pitcher or other easy-pouring vessel. Strain again through 2 new layers of cheesecloth into 1 large bottle or a number of small bottles or jars. I strongly suggest letting the Ginger Ice sit for 1 to 2 weeks in the freezer before serving. If you absolutely can't wait, shake well with ice and strain before serving.

A NOTE: Because this is so tasty chilled, and because the flavors continue to emerge in the freezer, be sure that when giving this liqueur as a gift, you add a note to this effect, so that whoever receives it can take full advantage.

The HOT HORSE

Makes 1½ pints

I f I could set the title to this wicked number in lights, as a way of warning, I would. Instead, let me just say that if you don't have a hankering for horseradish, this is one you'll want to avoid. All those whose chins dropped at hearing that there's a recipe for a horse-radish liqueur, please close your mouths. For those like me, who start smiling as the wasabi hits when eating sushi, it's a pleasure. The recipe comes from the inventive mind of my pal Jeremy Holt, who sometimes writes about food and drink under the Husky Boy moniker (check out thehuskyboy.blogspot.com), and who is one amazing liqueur maker.

3 ounces fresh horseradish, peeled and cut into large matchsticks

1½ cups grain alcohol or high-proof vodka

1½ cups water (see A Note)

1. Put the horseradish and grain alcohol in a glass container with a tight-fitting lid. Stir, seal, and place in a cool, dry spot away from sunlight. Let sit for 2 weeks.

2. Add the water, stir slightly, and reseal. Return to its spot. Let sit for 2 more weeks.

3. Strain through a double layer of cheese-cloth into a pitcher or other easy-pouring vessel. Strain again through 2 new layers of cheesecloth into 1 large bottle or a number of small bottles or jars. It will probably have a yellowish hue, a signal of its slightly fiery nature.

A NOTE: When adding the water, stay away from the tap unless you have a serious filter. Jeremy suggests Volvic bottled water, and since he came up with the recipe, I'd trust him.

A COCKTAIL SUGGESTION: Use this instead of plain vodka in a Bloody Mary. It's also great served ice-cold on its own.

Heroic HAZELNUT

Makes about 2¼ pints

Heroic Hazelnut isn't a hero in the real sense of the word; it won't, for example, pull you out from in front of an out-of-control bus. But it makes a lovely accompaniment for dessert at the end of a fall dinner, and it can assuredly turn around a dinner party that isn't going as perfectly as planned. It also rescues a dull cup of coffee, when added with a steady hand. And I think these small gestures elevate it to at least the lower rungs of heroism.

¾ pound skin-on raw hazelnuts (about 2½ cups)

2 cups vodka

1 cup brandy

1½ cups Simple Syrup (page 12)

1 teaspoon pure vanilla extract

1. Coarsely chop the hazelnuts. Put the hazelnuts, vodka, and brandy in a glass container with a tight-fitting lid. Stir well and seal. Place the container in a cool, dry spot away from sunlight. Let sit for 3 weeks, swirling occasionally.

2. Add the simple syrup and vanilla, stir, and reseal. Return to its spot. Let sit for 2 more weeks.

3. Strain the liqueur through a double layer of cheesecloth into a pitcher or other easy-pouring vessel. Strain again through 2 new layers of cheesecloth into 1 large bottle or a number of small bottles or jars. Once bottled, let the liqueur sit for 2 more weeks before serving.

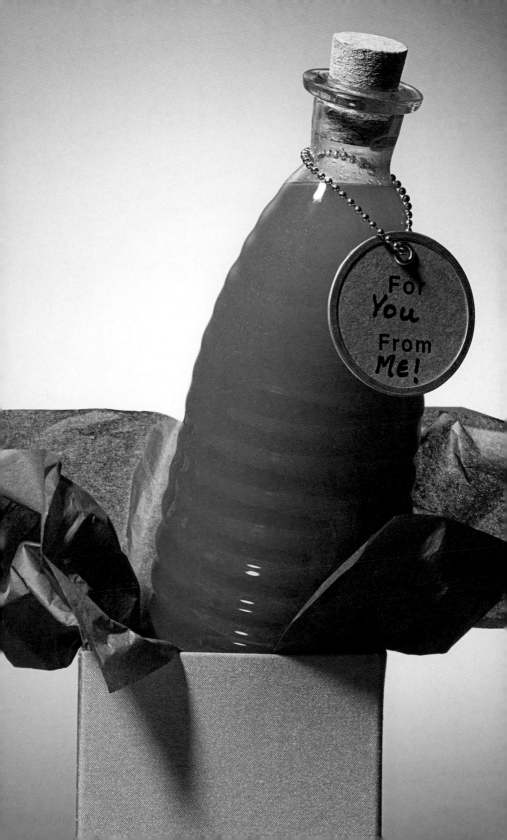

For
You
From
Me!

MILLEFIORI

Makes about 2¾ pints

I taly is famous for its liqueurs, with good reason. I was overwhelmingly happy when I discovered in a Florence bookstore (feel free to be jealous) a lovely little Italian book by Davide Longo called *Come Fare Liquori e Grappe di Erbe e Frutta*, which translates into "How to Make Liqueurs and Grappas with Herbs and Fruit." This recipe for Millefiori ("thousand flowers") is adapted from the book, and demonstrates how intricate a liqueur can be. The taste, layered and spicy and distinctive, shows why tracking down the ingredients is well worth it. Appreciate this on its own, chilled or at room temperature.

2 tablespoons whole coriander seeds

4 or 5 fresh mint leaves

½ teaspoon ground cardamom

½ teaspoon whole cloves

½ teaspoon freshly grated lemon zest

½ teaspoon ground mace

½ teaspoon fresh marjoram leaves

½ teaspoon fresh thyme leaves

4 cups vodka

1½ cups Simple Syrup (page 12)

1. Grind the coriander seeds and mint leaves with a mortar and pestle. You don't want to destroy them, but do want them broken up.

2. Put the coriander-mint combo, cardamom, cloves, lemon zest, mace, marjoram, thyme, and vodka in a glass container with a tight-fitting lid. Stir well and seal. Place in a cool, dry spot away from sunlight. Let sit for 2 weeks, swirling it every couple of days.

3. Add the simple syrup, stir well, and reseal. Return to its spot. Let sit for 2 weeks, swirling every couple of days.

4. Filter the liquid through a fine-mesh strainer into a bowl. Carefully strain through a double layer of cheesecloth into a pitcher or other easy-pouring vessel. Finally, strain through 2 new layers of cheesecloth into another pitcher or bottle. Check that the liqueur is free of debris. If it isn't, repeat this step until the desired clarity is reached. Pour the liqueur into 1 large bottle or a number of small bottles or jars.

MINTY *Fresh*

Makes about 2¼ pints

Because this liqueur sounds a bit like a toothpaste tagline, you may be tempted to do away with brushing and just rinse your pearly whites with Minty Fresh instead. I understand the impulse—who wouldn't want an excuse to have another snifter of this bracing drink? Here's a compromise: Continue brushing your teeth (twice daily), and have a little bit of this on top of a scoop of vanilla ice cream, or just sip it chilled. That way, both you and your dentist will remain happy.

1½ cups loosely packed fresh mint leaves

3 cups vodka

2 cups Simple Syrup (page 12)

1. Wash the mint leaves and dry completely on towels. Put the leaves in a glass container with a tight-fitting lid. Using a muddler or wooden spoon, mash the mint against the bottom of the container. You don't need to completely destroy it, but give it a fairly good pounding.

2. Add the vodka and stir well. Seal and place the bottle in a dry, cool spot away from sunlight. Let sit for 2 weeks, swirling at least every other day.

3. Add the simple syrup, stir, and reseal. Return to its spot. Let sit for 2 more weeks, again swirling every other day.

4. Strain the liqueur through a double layer of cheesecloth into a pitcher or other easy-pouring vessel. Strain again through 2 new layers of cheesecloth into 1 large bottle or a number of small bottles or jars. Served chilled.

A NOTE: If you just don't think this is as green as a mint liqueur should be, add ½ teaspoon of green food coloring to the pitcher in step 4.

A COCKTAIL SUGGESTION: Minty Fresh adds that bright mint touch to a Stinger. Just combine 1½ ounces brandy and 1½ ounces Minty Fresh in a cocktail shaker filled with ice. Shake well and strain into a cocktail glass.

Uncovering
THE EXOTICS

C alling all hunters, explorers, and expeditioners, all adventuresome sorts: I'm here to talk about stalking the exotic liqueurs. Sometimes you have to travel to distant lands (or distant grocery stores), tread lightly, be watchful, and then wait before pouncing and pouring these exotic liquid beauties. Of course, your dedication equals treasures far beyond the everyday—liqueurs that might test you a little (such as A Bitter Brew), but for which you'll eventually fall head-over-heels (as demonstrated by the Love Liqueur).

Amaro
A Bitter Brew
Caribbean Queen
Lebaoku
Love Liqueur
Persephonia
Scotch Treat
October Prescription
Pa Pa Papaya

AMARO

Makes about 2 1/4 pints

T he word "amaro" refers to a whole genre of Italian after-dinner liqueurs, or *digestivos*, with a bittersweet balance that is intended to aid digestion. I've enjoyed a variety of amaros in Italy and elsewhere (many brands are exported), and I hope that this recipe lives up to their high standards, both as a taste sensation, with rich herbal overtones, and as a preferred chilled or room-temperature solo sip after one bite too many of delicious food.

¾ teaspoon whole anise seeds

1 teaspoon fresh sage leaves

1 teaspoon fresh rosemary leaves

½ teaspoon gentian root (see A Note)

½ teaspoon whole cloves

3 cups grain alcohol or high-proof vodka

1½ cups Simple Syrup (page 12)

1. Using a mortar and pestle, grind the anise, sage, rosemary, gentian, and cloves. When well ground, put them in a glass container with a tight-fitting lid.

2. Add the grain alcohol and stir. Seal with a nod to all the great amaros worldwide. Place in a cool, dry spot away from sunlight. Let sit for 3 weeks, swirling the contents occasionally.

3. Add the simple syrup, stir, and reseal. Return to its spot. Let sit for 3 more weeks, stopping by occasionally to swirl it.

4. Strain the liqueur through a double layer of cheesecloth into a pitcher or other easy-pouring vessel. Strain again through 2 new layers of cheesecloth into another pitcher or bottle. If it's still cloudy, repeat this step until it's clear. Pour the liqueur into 1 large bottle or a number of small bottles or jars.

A NOTE: Gentian, a bitter herb, is available at good natural foods stores or online at dandelionbotanical.com.

A Bitter BREW

Makes about 1¾ pints

A Bitter Brew is, indeed, bitter, though not without a hint of sweetness. If you generally don't like the bitter-er liqueurs, though, chances are this won't thrill you. If you do, here's your recipe. It uses angelica, an aromatic and slightly bitter plant root. It's available at better natural foods stores and online at dandelionbotanical.com.

1 medium to large orange

½ cup loosely packed fresh mint leaves

½ teaspoon chopped angelica root

2 teaspoons gentian root (see page 66)

¼ teaspoon whole anise seeds

½ teaspoon chopped peeled fresh ginger

½ teaspoon whole cloves

3 cups brandy

½ cup Simple Syrup (page 12)

1. Wash, dry, and peel the orange, trimming away any white pith. Put the peel in a glass container with a tight-fitting lid.

2. Using a mortar and pestle, grind the mint, angelica, gentian, anise, ginger, and cloves. When well ground, add them to the orange peel.

3. Add the brandy and stir slightly. Seal and place in a cool, dry spot away from sunlight. Let sit for 2 weeks, swirling every third day or thereabouts.

4. Add the simple syrup, stir again, and reseal. Return to its spot. Let sit for I month (this long sitting will really make it bitter), swirling again every 3 to 4 days.

5. Strain the liqueur through a double layer of cheesecloth into a pitcher or other easy-pouring vessel. Strain again through 2 new layers of cheesecloth into another pitcher or bottle. If there are still bits of herbs floating around, repeat this step until it's clear. Pour the liqueur into I large bottle or a number of small bottles or jars.

A SERVING SUGGESTION: I enjoy my Bitter Brew served solo at room temperature, but it's also dandy chilled or mixed with club soda over ice.

CARIBBEAN *Queen*

Makes about 2¼ pints

Billy Ocean may not be everyone's cup of rum-based liqueur (those who believe that wearing all black every day, even in summer, is truly comfortable, for example). I hope that most can at least enjoy this liqueur that shares a name with one of his biggest hits, though. If they can't, well, you wouldn't have to have them over, anyway.

2 medium to large oranges

1 lime

1 cup freshly grated coconut (see page 84)

1 cup chopped fresh mango

3 cups white rum

1½ cups Simple Syrup (page 12)

1. Wash, dry, and peel the oranges and lime, trimming away any white pith. Put the peels, coconut, and mango in a glass container with a tight-fitting lid. (Either eat any leftover fruit or juice it and combine it with ice, rum, and simple syrup for a sweet drink.)

2. Add the rum, stir, and seal. Place in a cool, dry spot away from sunlight. Let sit for 2 weeks, swirling occasionally.

3. Add the simple syrup, stir, and reseal. Return to its spot. Let sit for 2 more weeks, swirling occasionally.

4. Filter the liqueur through a fine-mesh strainer into a bowl. Strain again through a double layer of cheesecloth into a pitcher or other easy-pouring vessel. Finally, strain through 2 new layers of cheesecloth into I large bottle or a number of small bottles or jars.

A SERVING SUGGESTION: The CQ is best icy cold on its own, or mixed with a lot of shaved ice, orange juice, and a little lime juice.

LEBAOKU

Makes about 2 ½ pints

This liqueur's mystical moniker comes from the main ingredients, lemongrass and Thai basil. These intriguing flavors are why you must serve this with the proper mysterious flair, speaking in a low voice with an unidentifiable accent. The Asian influences make Lebaoku an off-the-beaten-path gift, too, and demand that if giving it away, you make a small kimono for the bottle to wear. Serve this chilled on its own.

1 cup loosely packed fresh Thai basil leaves

2½ cups vodka

¼ cup diced lemongrass (see A Note)

1½ cups sugar

1¼ cups water

1. Wash and dry the basil leaves. Put the basil and vodka in a glass container with a tight-fitting lid. Swirl briefly to make sure the basil is covered. Seal and place the container in a cool, dry spot away from sunlight. Let it sit for 2 weeks, swirling occasionally.

2. Put the lemongrass, sugar, and water in a medium-size saucepan over medium heat. Bring the mixture almost to a boil, stirring regularly. Don't let the mixture boil, but cook until the sugar is completely dissolved. Remove from the heat and let cool completely.

3. Add the lemongrass mixture to the vodka-basil mixture, stir once to combine, and reseal. Return to its spot. Let sit for 2 more weeks.

4. Strain the liqueur through a double layer of cheesecloth into a pitcher or other easy-pouring vessel. Strain again through 2 new layers of cheesecloth into 1 large bottle or a number of small bottles or jars. If you can possibly resist, place the Lebaoku in the freezer and don't taste for at least another week.

A NOTE: You'll want only to use the rooty thicker part of the lemongrass, not the leafier part. Cut off the hard end, and then pull off the first two outer layers. The softer inner layers have more fragrance and flavor.

LOVE *Liqueur*

Makes about 3 pints

This recipe is adapted from Pattie Vargas and Rich Gulling's *Cordials from Your Kitchen* (Storey Publishing, 1997), a boon for any connoisseur of homemade liqueurs. The main ingredient here is coriander, a key ingredient in love potions back in the day (in this case, the Middle Ages and Renaissance). This isn't to say that a particular person will fall in your direction when served a glass—but it certainly won't hurt romantic matters.

2 cups water

2 cups honey

1 tablespoon whole coriander seeds

1 piece star anise

½ teaspoon dried rose hips

2 tablespoons dried hibiscus flowers

1 tablespoon freshly grated orange zest

1 cup high-proof vodka or grain alcohol

1 cup brandy

1. Combine the water and honey in a saucepan, and bring the mixture to a boil over medium-high heat. Boil for about 2 minutes. Skim off any foam, and remove the saucepan from the heat. Let cool completely.

2. While the honey syrup is cooling, grind the coriander, star anise, and rose hips with a mortar and pestle. Once fairly well ground, put them in a glass container with a tight-fitting lid. Add the hibiscus flowers, orange zest, vodka, and brandy. Stir well.

3. Add the cooled syrup and stir again. Seal and place in a cool, dry spot away from sunlight. Let sit for 1 month, swirling occasionally.

4. Strain the liqueur through a double layer of cheesecloth into a pitcher or other easy-pouring vessel. Strain again through 2 new layers of cheesecloth into another pitcher or bottle. If there are still lots of herb pieces floating around, repeat this step until it's clear. Pour the liqueur into 1 large bottle or a number of small bottles or jars.

A NOTE: Look for rose hips and dried hibiscus flowers in natural foods stores, specialty herb stores, and online at dandelionbotanical.com.

PERSEPHONIA

Makes about 1½ pints

I don't think there's any danger that you'll suffer Persephone's fate when partaking of this pomegranate-based liqueur (namely, that for every sip you take you'll have to spend a month with Hades in his domain), so drink freely. The only real thing to worry about is the seeding of the fruits (I suggest using a spoon to pop them out)—and making the decision that it's okay to share.

2 pomegranates

1 tablespoon freshly grated orange zest

½ teaspoon ground cinnamon

2 cups vodka

½ cup Simple Syrup (page 12)

1. Remove the seeds from the pomegranates using a spoon or any other process you think works best. Put the seeds in a bowl and, using a muddler or wooden spoon, crush them to release the juice.

2. Put the juice and seed bits, orange zest, cinnamon, and vodka in a glass container with a tight-fitting lid. Seal and place the container in a cool, dry, place away from sunlight. Let sit for 2 weeks, swirling occasionally.

3. Add the simple syrup, stir, and reseal. Return to its spot. Let sit for 2 more weeks.

4. Carefully strain the liqueur through a double layer of cheesecloth into a pitcher or other easy-pouring vessel. Strain again through 2 new layers of cheesecloth into another pitcher or bottle. Check that the liqueur is free of debris (the little seed particles can slip through). If it isn't, repeat this step until it is. Pour the liqueur into 1 large bottle or a number of small bottles or jars.

A COCKTAIL SUGGESTION: If the sun's shining bright, try pouring 1½ ounces over ice in a highball glass. Top with club soda (if you're not feeling sweet) or 7UP (if you are, a little).

SCOTCH *Treat*

Makes about 1¾ pints

T hough the band is Irish, and the base of this liqueur is Scotch, I still always feel like singing Thin Lizzy's "Whiskey in the Jar" when drinking this one. Maybe it's just one of the later lines in the song, "but I takes delight in the juice of the barley," or maybe the adventure-style narrative of the lyrics, which match the rustic nature of this mixture. I'm not saying you need to dress up as an antique soldier of fortune and run across the hills swilling and singing, but I'm not saying you shouldn't, either.

½ teaspoon whole fennel seeds

½ teaspoon whole caraway seeds

2 teaspoons fresh sage leaves

2 cups Scotch whisky

1½ cups Simple Syrup (page 12)

1. Using a mortar and pestle, mash the fennel, caraway, and sage. Put this mixture into a glass container with a tight-fitting lid.

2. Add the Scotch and stir well. Seal and place in a cool, dry spot away from sunlight. Let sit for 3 weeks, swirling occasionally.

3. Add the simple syrup, stir again, and reseal. Return to its spot. Let sit for 3 more weeks, swirling occasionally.

4. Carefully strain the liqueur through a double layer of cheesecloth into a pitcher or other easy-pouring vessel. Strain again through 2 new layers of cheesecloth into 1 large bottle or a number of small bottles or jars. Let sit for 1 more week before serving.

A NOTE: I suggest using a solid blended Scotch, like Johnny Walker, Cutty Sark, or J & B.

OCTOBER *Prescription*

Makes about 3½ pints

I t can be so difficult to shift out of late summer mode, but October quickly gets colder and darker. There is a way around this fall failing, and that's to embrace the October Prescription. It takes fall darlings apple and cinnamon and adds a few new spicy wrinkles that are sure to sparkle taste buds and attitudes—as long as you remember to make it near the beginning of September, so it's ready in time.

2 cups dark brown
sugar

3 cups apple juice

1½ teaspoons
ground cinnamon

1 teaspoon ground
nutmeg

¼ teaspoon whole
cloves

2 cups brandy

1 teaspoon pure
vanilla extract

1. Combine the brown sugar and apple juice in a medium-size saucepan over medium heat and bring almost, but not quite, to a boil, stirring regularly. Once it's reached this almost-boiling point, reduce the heat and cook for 5 minutes.

2. Add the cinnamon, nutmeg, and cloves. Cook for 5 minutes more, stirring regularly and never letting the liquid get above a simmer. Remove from the heat and let cool completely.

3. Pour the mixture into a glass container with a tight-fitting lid. Add the brandy and seal. Place in a cool, dry spot away from sunlight. Let sit for 2 weeks, swirling occasionally.

4. Add the vanilla, stir well, and reseal. Return to its spot. Let sit for 2 more weeks.

5. Strain the liqueur through a double layer of cheesecloth into a pitcher or other easy-pouring vessel. Strain again through 2 new layers of cheesecloth into 1 large bottle or a number of small bottles or jars.

A NOTE: The October Prescription can be enjoyed at room temperature, or even slightly heated, as well as chilled. It's also good when added to a mug of warm apple cider.

Pa Pa PAPAYA

Makes about 2 ½ pints

I f you want to retitle this mix "fruta bomba," go right ahead (as the papaya is sometimes called the same), but be prepared in advance for folks resorting to colloquialisms like "this is the bomba" or "you're the bomba for serving this bomba." Serve on a warm day so as not to miss out on the tropical nature and summertime style of the Pa Pa Papaya.

1 medium-size
papaya

2 limes

1 tablespoon
chopped peeled
fresh ginger

3 cups dark rum

2 cups Simple
Syrup (page 12)

1. Using a sharp peeler or paring knife, remove the skin from the papaya. Cut the fruit in half lengthwise, cut the ends off, and remove the seeds with a spoon. Cut the papaya flesh into chunks. (You should have approximately 4 cups.) Put the papaya chunks in a glass container with a tight-fitting lid.

2. Wash, dry, and peel the limes, trimming away any white pith. Add the lime peel and ginger to the papaya. (Use the limes as you will.) Using a muddler or wooden spoon, muddle the papaya, ginger, and lime well.

3. Add the rum and stir forcefully but smoothly. Seal and place in a cool, dry spot away from sunlight. Let sit for 2 weeks, swirling occasionally.

4. Add the simple syrup, stir, and reseal. Return to its spot. Let sit for 2 weeks, swirling occasionally.

5. Filter the liqueur through a fine-mesh strainer into a bowl. Strain again through a double layer of cheesecloth into a pitcher or other easy-pouring vessel. Finally, strain through 2 new layers of cheesecloth into 1 large bottle or a number of small bottles or jars.

A COCKTAIL SUGGESTION: Pour 1½ ounces over ice in a highball glass and top it off with cold Sprite or 7UP and a lime slice. Or if that sounds too sugary, go half-and-half with cold club soda and Sprite or 7UP—call it a Papaya Press.

For the **SWEET-TOOTH SIPPER**

Now, each and every one of the sweet-tooths in the audience: Quit being shy, forget about hiding those cravings, and step right up to the front of the line (and the start of this chapter). The liqueurs contained here are designed for those of you who dream about dessert, who always carry a spare candy bar in the car, and who look at rows of chocolates with an ear-to-ear smile. Embrace your sugary side, embrace the following recipes, and everyone goes home happy.

Advocaat
Enticing Amaretto
Butterscotch
Chocolate Mint
Crazy for Coconut
Eggsala
Irish Cream Liqueur
Chocolate Cream Liqueur
Sweet Macadamiana
Coffee Liqueur

ADVOCAAT

Makes about 1¾ to 2 pints

Proving that anything can be made into liqueur by the truly creative human mind, Advocaat was originally made by Dutch settlers in South America using whipped avocado. When taking the mix back to the Netherlands (a spot which, at least at the time, wasn't known for its avocado crop), eggs were subbed in for the avocado with delicious results. The modern version remains egg based.

8 egg yolks, from fresh organic eggs

1½ cups Simple Syrup (page 12)

2 cups brandy

1 teaspoon pure vanilla extract

1. Put the egg yolks in a blender. Start blending on low, and slowly drizzle in the simple syrup. Once all the syrup has been added, blend on a low for another 5 seconds.

2. Scrape the sides of the blender if needed. Start it again on a low speed, and slowly pour the brandy into the egg-syrup mixture. Once the brandy has been added, do the same with the vanilla. When all the ingredients are in, blend on low speed for 5 more seconds.

3. Pour the mixture into 1 large bottle or a number of small bottles or jars. Seal and refrigerate. Let sit for 1 week to let the flavors blend, and consume within 2 weeks after that.

A WARNING: This liqueur contains raw eggs, so don't serve it to anyone with a compromised immune system.

A NOTE: As separation can occur over time, you'll probably want to shake this well before drinking. If you want to increase the stability of the emulsification, add a teaspoon of lecithin when mixing. I avoid the lecithin (which you can buy online or in vitamin stores), but then, I don't mind shaking.

A COCKTAIL SUGGESTION: There are a number of Advocaat drinks, including the Bombardino, which mixes 1 ounce of this with 1 ounce whiskey in a mug of hot coffee. This is guaranteed to warm up a winter's day.

Enticing AMARETTO

Makes about 2 ¾ pints

A maretto is an Italian liqueur made from almonds, a sweet mixture (even though the name is a derivation of *amaro,* which means "bitter") that's taken on a bit of a romantic mystique. That doesn't mean that simply serving this to a potential paramour will result in love and happiness. However, neither will it hurt your case.

1 cup skin-on whole raw almonds

1 tablespoon freshly grated orange zest

2½ cups brandy

1 cup granulated sugar

1 cup light brown sugar

1½ cups water

1 tablespoon pure vanilla extract

1. Coarsely chop the almonds. Put them, the orange zest, and the brandy in a glass container with a tight-fitting lid. Stir well. Seal and place the container in a cool, dry spot away from sunlight. Let sit for 2 weeks, swirling occasionally.

2. Combine the sugars and water in a medium-size saucepan over medium-high heat. Stirring occasionally, bring the mixture to a boil. Lower the heat a bit, keeping the mixture at a low boil for 5 minutes. Turn off the heat, and let the syrup completely cool in the pan. This step can be done anytime during the 2 weeks mentioned in step I, as long as the syrup is refrigerated until it's added to the liqueur.

3. Add the syrup and vanilla to the brandy, stir well, and reseal. Return to its spot. Let sit for 2 more weeks, swirling at least every other day.

4. Carefully strain the liqueur through a double layer of cheesecloth into a pitcher or other easy-pouring vessel. Strain again through 2 new layers of cheesecloth into I large bottle or a number of small bottles or jars.

A SERVING SUGGESTION: Serve chilled or at room temperature, depending on your mood.

BUTTERSCOTCH

Makes about 1¾ pints

I t's good, I think, to avoid overuse of flavoring extracts, but sometimes you have to go that route, such as with this Butterscotch liqueur—and really, the results are darn tasty. If you didn't use the extract, this recipe probably wouldn't be made at all, and that would be a shame, because it's so worthwhile.

2 cups vodka

1½ cups Simple Syrup (page 12)

1 teaspoon butterscotch extract

1. Combine everything in a glass container with a tight-fitting lid. Stir well. Seal the container and place it in a cool, dry spot away from sunlight. Let sit for 3 weeks.

2. Carefully pour the liqueur into 1 large bottle or a number of small bottles or jars. This is best when chilled, so either store in the freezer or shake with ice and strain before serving.

A NOTE: To find butterscotch extract, check baking-supply stores, specialty grocers, or online.

A COCKTAIL SUGGESTION: Combine 2½ ounces Butterscotch with ½ ounce crème de cacao to make a Butterfinger. When someone tries to sneak a taste, remember to say, "Don't lay a finger on my Butterfinger."

A QUOTE: "But Sterne is not a drink or a wine either of barley or grape—he is a liqueur—agreeable, but not perhaps exactly wholesome."
—Laurence Sterne, *A Sentimental Journey through France and Italy*

CHOCOLATE *Mint*
Makes about 3 pints

A ll that's needed to complete a perfectly romantic evening is a delightful sip of this after-dinner cordial. Once you reveal to your sipping companion that you actually made, with your own two hands, the charming tipple being consumed, the romance meter will head even higher. While tasty at room temperature, this is best chilled.

1½ cups loosely packed fresh mint leaves

3 cups vodka

½ cup granulated sugar

1½ cups light brown sugar

1½ cups water

1 teaspoon chocolate extract

¼ teaspoon pure vanilla extract

1. Wash and dry the mint leaves. Put the leaves in a glass container with a tight-fitting lid. Using a muddler or wooden spoon, slightly crush the mint leaves. Add the vodka, stir, and seal. Place in a cool, dry spot away from sunlight. Let sit for I week.

2. Combine the sugars and water in a medium-size saucepan over medium-high heat. Stirring occasionally, bring the mixture just to a boil. Lower the heat a bit, keeping the mixture at a low boil for 5 minutes. Turn off the heat, and let the syrup cool completely in the pan. This step can be done anytime during the week mentioned in step I, as long as the syrup is refrigerated until it's added to the liqueur.

3. Add the syrup and chocolate and vanilla extracts to the vodka, stir well, and reseal. Return to its spot. Let sit for 2 more weeks, swirling at least every other day.

4. Carefully strain the liqueur through a double layer of cheesecloth into a pitcher or other easy-pouring vessel. Strain again through 2 new layers of cheesecloth into I large bottle or a number of small bottles or jars.

Crazy for COCONUT
Makes 1¾ to 2 pints

G o coconutty via this rum-based concoction—but not until after you've grated the coconut, as the process can be a little dangerous. Using bagged grated coconut isn't fun either— the end result doesn't taste nearly as good as when fresh is used.

2 cups freshly grated coconut (see A Note)

2 cups white rum

1¾ cups Simple Syrup (page 12)

1. Put the coconut and rum in a glass container with a tight-fitting lid. Stir slightly, seal, and place in a cool, dry spot away from sunlight. Let sit for 2 weeks, swirling gently every other day.

2. Add the simple syrup, stir briefly, and reseal. Return to its spot. Let sit for 2 more weeks, swirling the contents every other day (a little less gently this time).

3. Carefully strain the liqueur through a double layer of cheesecloth into a pitcher or other easy-pouring vessel. Strain again through 2 new layers of cheesecloth into I large bottle or a number of small bottles or jars.

A NOTE: Here's how to deal with a whole coconut: Use a hammer and nail (really) to make holes in the soft dimples of the coconut. Let the juice drain out over a bowl. Place the coconut on a kitchen towel and, firmly but carefully, use the hammer to crack it open and into smaller pieces (you might want to do this outside, to avoid damaging your counter). Grate the flesh using the smaller holes of a box grater, grating in as little of the brown skin as possible.

A COCKTAIL SUGGESTION: Pour 2 ounces of this over ice in a highball glass. Add 2 ounces of pineapple juice. Top it off with ginger ale and call it a Coconut PG. This liqueur is also a treat served ice-cold by itself, with a squeeze of lime. And it pairs smoothly with ice cream.

A QUOTE: "Here was a clue worth having. Poirot delicately dipped his finger into the liquid, and tasted it gingerly. He made a grimace. 'Coco— with—I think—rum in it.'"
—Agatha Christie, *The Mysterious Affair at Styles*

EGGSALA

Makes about 2 1/2 pints

This delight is a variation on an egg liqueur recipe I found in Dona and Mel Meilach's handy and enjoyable book, *Homemade Liqueurs* (Contemporary Books, 1979). It's delish, as much dessert in a way as a drink—which makes it doubly fine to pair with a dessert, because then it's like you're getting to have two desserts. I'm having trouble typing just thinking about it.

6 egg yolks

1¾ cups light brown sugar

1 cup milk

½ teaspoon pure vanilla extract

1½ cups Marsala

1 cup brandy

1. Beat the egg yolks until well combined. Put them and the sugar in a medium-size nonstick saucepan over medium-low heat. While stirring, slowly add the milk. Still stirring, slowly add the vanilla and ³⁄₄ cup of the Marsala. Raise the heat to medium, and stir continually. Once all lumps are dissolved and everything is cozy, simmer for 5 minutes, while stirring—be sure it doesn't get too hot, as you want to avoid scorching at all costs.

2. Remove the almost-Eggsala from the heat and let cool to room temperature, stirring occasionally. Add the remainder of the wine and the brandy and stir well to combine.

3. Pour into a glass container with a tight-fitting lid. Seal, shake well, and refrigerate. Let sit for 1 week, shaking it every day for good measure.

4. Leave it in the container or pour it into smaller containers. Keep in the fridge and consume within 1 month.

IRISH CREAM *Liqueur*

Makes about 2½ pints

Thdis luscious treat is a holiday hit—it delightfully matches the festive spirit—perfect as a warming dessert drink and also a good idea for gifts, even if the gift is only for yourself. I had it first when a bottle was given to me and my wife by Tara Vodopich, who is herself as bubbly as a holiday punch.

One 14-ounce can sweetened condensed milk

1⅔ cups Irish whiskey

1 cup light cream

2 tablespoons chocolate syrup

1 teaspoon instant coffee granules

1 teaspoon pure vanilla extract

1 teaspoon almond extract

1. Put all of the ingredients in any order you want in a sturdy blender. Blend on medium for 1 minute, making sure that everything is completely combined.

2. Pour the mixture into 1 large (at least 1½ liters) bottle or a number of smaller bottles or jars with tight-fitting lids. Seal and refrigerate before using (it can also be placed in the freezer, but it might get slushy). You can serve this right away, and please consume within 2 weeks.

A COCKTAIL SUGGESTION: If want to relive your college days with a silly-named beverage, float ½ ounce of this liqueur over equal parts Kahlúa and Crown Royal. You'll be drinking a Duck Fart. Irish Cream Liqueur is also fine (and more elegant) sipped solo after dinner, and a generous spoonful drizzled over a hot brownie is sure to bring smiles.

Chocolate **CREAM LIQUEUR**
Makes about 2½ pints

D o I need to say that 1 or 2 ounces of this creamy creation added to coffee turns a cuppa joe into a cuppa joy? Do I even need to remind you that, since this has cream and milk in it, it needs to be refrigerated after making it? I'm guessing the answer to the first question is "no" and the second is "no, that's obvious," but you can never be too sure.

2 cups dark rum

One 14-ounce can sweetened condensed milk

1 cup heavy cream

½ cup chocolate syrup

½ teaspoon pure vanilla extract

1 teaspoon coconut extract

1. Put all of the ingredients in order (you want the rum to take the first plunge, to convince the other ingredients everything is okay) in a sturdy blender. Blend on high for 1 minute, until smooth and well combined.

2. Pour the liqueur into 1 large bottle or a number of smaller bottles or jars with tight-fitting lids. Seal and refrigerate. You can serve this right away, and please consume within 2 weeks.

A NOTE: I suggest shaking the bottle in a serious manner before serving (unless you're serving right after making it) to assure that no settling has occurred.

A COCKTAIL SUGGESTION: Combine 1 ounce Chocolate Cream Liqueur and 2 ounces vodka in a cocktail shaker with ice, shake well, and strain into a cocktail glass. Garnish with a candy cane and you'll have a holiday party highlight.

Sweet MACADAMIANA

Makes about 2 ½ pints

T his island-style infusion of macadamia nuts and vodka results in a liqueur that could be sipped happily solo over ice, with a taste that won't disappoint candy lovers but that has enough layering and nutty flavoring to avoid being cloying.

One 6-ounce jar
roasted unsalted
macadamia nuts
(about 1½ cups)

2 cups vodka

¾ cup honey

2 cups dark brown
sugar

1½ cups water

1. Coarsely chop the macadamia nuts. Put the nuts and vodka in a glass container with a tight-fitting lid. Seal and place the container in a cool, dry spot away from sunlight. Let sit for 2 weeks, twirling (like a hula dancer, but more briskly) once every day or two.

2. Combine the honey, sugar, and water in a medium-size saucepan over medium-high heat. Stirring occasionally, bring the mixture almost to a boil. Lower the heat a bit, keeping the mixture at a low simmer for 5 minutes. Remove from the heat and let cool completely in the pan. This step can be done anytime during the 2 weeks mentioned in step 1, as long as the syrup is refrigerated until it's added to the liqueur.

3. Add the syrup to the vodka, stir well, and reseal. Return to its spot. Let sit for 2 more weeks, twirling at least every other day.

4. Carefully strain the liqueur through a double layer of cheesecloth into a pitcher or other easy-pouring vessel. Strain again through 2 new layers of cheesecloth into 1 large bottle or a number of small bottles or jars. Let sit for 1 more week before partaking.

A COCKTAIL SUGGESTION: Shake 2 ounces Sweet Macadamiana and 1 ounce cream with ice and strain into a cocktail glass (add 1 ounce crème de cacao if you're of a chocolate-loving bent). For something a little stronger, combine 2 ounces bourbon, 1 ounce Sweet Macadamiana, and ice in an old-fashioned glass. Either way, you'll be whistling a Don Ho song in no time.

COFFEE *Liqueur*

Makes about 3 pints

This variation on Kahlúa has a more pronounced coffee taste, and it can sub in for that well-known brand in most situations, which means that an ounce added to a cup of a coffee perks up any brunch or brings sophistication to post-dinner conversation.

¼ cup instant espresso powder

2½ cups light brown sugar

1 cup water

¼ cup whole coffee beans of your choice

3 cups brandy

1 teaspoon pure vanilla extract

1. Combine the instant espresso, sugar, and water in a medium-size saucepan over medium-high heat. Stirring occasionally, bring the mixture almost to a boil. Lower the heat a bit, keeping the mixture at a low simmer for 5 minutes. Turn off the heat, and let the syrup cool completely in the pan.

2. Put the syrup, coffee beans, and brandy in a glass container with a tight-fitting lid. Stir well. Seal and place the container in a cool, dry spot away from sunlight. Let sit for 2 weeks, swirling occasionally.

3. Add the vanilla, stir again, and reseal. Return to its spot. Let sit for 2 more weeks.

4. Carefully strain the liqueur through a double layer of cheesecloth into a pitcher or other easy-pouring vessel. Strain again through 2 new layers of cheesecloth into 1 large bottle or a number of small bottles or jars.

A COCKTAIL SUGGESTION: For a knockout Black Russian, pour 1½ ounces Coffee Liqueur and 2 ounces vodka over ice in an old-fashioned glass. Stir a couple of times and you'll be dreaming of Moscow.

MEASUREMENT *Equivalents*

Please note that all conversions are approximate.

LIQUID CONVERSIONS

U.S.	IMPERIAL	METRIC
1 tsp	—	5 ml
1 tbs	½ fl oz	15 ml
2 tbs	1 fl oz	30 ml
3 tbs	1½ fl oz	45 ml
¼ cup	2 fl oz	60 ml
⅓ cup	2½ fl oz	75 ml
⅓ cup + 1 tbs	3 fl oz	90 ml
⅓ cup + 2 tbs	3½ fl oz	100 ml
½ cup	4 fl oz	120 ml
⅓ cup	5 fl oz	150 ml
¾ cup	6 fl oz	180 ml
¾ cup + 2 tbs	7 fl oz	200 ml
1 cup	8 fl oz	240 ml
1 cup + 2 tbs	9 fl oz	275 ml
1¼ cups	10 fl oz	300 ml
1⅓ cups	11 fl oz	325 ml
1½ cups	12 fl oz	350 ml
1⅔ cups	13 fl oz	375 ml
1¾ cups	14 fl oz	400 ml
1¾ cups + 2 tbs	15 fl oz	450 ml
2 cups (1 pint)	16 fl oz	475 ml
2½ cups	20 fl oz	600 ml
3 cups	24 fl oz	720 ml
4 cups (1 quart)	32 fl oz	945 ml

(1,000 ml is 1 liter)

INDEX

Note: *Italicized* page numbers refer to photographs.

ABOUT THE AUTHOR

A seasoned party host and master mixologist, A.J. Rathbun is the author of *Good Spirits* (winner of an IACP Cookbook Award), as well as *Party Drinks!* and a collection of poetry, *Want.* He has worked as a bartender, a waiter, a rock-band roadie, the director of the Poetry After Hours Program at the Seattle Art Museum, and more. A.J. lives in Seattle and invites you to visit his website at www.ajrathbun.com, where you can check out sample recipes, view the drink video of the month, and read about his other books.